Pastoral Administration

Pastoral Administration

Integrating Ministry and Management in the Church

DAVID S. LUECKE
&
SAMUEL SOUTHARD

WORD BOOKS
PUBLISHER
WACO, TEXAS

A DIVISION OF
WORD, INCORPORATED

PASTORAL ADMINISTRATION:
Integrating Management and Ministry in the Church

Unless otherwise indicated, Scripture quotations are from the Revised Standard Version of the Bible, copyrighted 1946, 1952, 1971, 1973 by the Division of Christian Education of the National Council of the Churches of Christ in the U.S.A., and are used by permission. Scripture quotations identified NKJV are from the New King James Version, copyright © 1979, 1980, 1982, Thomas Nelson, Inc., Publishers.

Library of Congress Cataloging in Publication Data

Luecke, David S., 1940–
  Pastoral administration.

  Bibliography: p.
  Includes index.
  1. Church management.   2. Pastoral theology.
I. Southard, Samuel.   II. Title.
BV652.L84   1986   254   86–11163

ISBN 0–8499–0558–3

67898 BKC 987654321

Printed in the United States of America

To my father, Rev. Edgar M. Luecke, who taught me pastoral administration by example before I knew it as a discipline to be studied.

DAVID S. LUECKE

To Donna and the members of the Santa Monica Vineyard who demonstrate the life of the Spirit in an organized body of Christ.

SAMUEL SOUTHARD

Contents

6 CONTENTS

Foreword

Management—it seems everyone wants to be in on it except ministers. Everyone? The evidence of the polls suggests that collegians line up today as never before to enter management. They seek business degrees because money, status, and fulfillment are supposed to come with management. Of course, trouble is ahead. The nation also needs physicists and engineers and school teachers, but at the moment, they are not forthcoming in numbers to match those of managers-to-be. More trouble—there are already too many managers. Someone has to "be managed," but not many are left in a world of managers. Economist Peter Drucker says that the management ranks are nearly full and will be for decades to come.

Management ranks in ministry are not full, if by this we mean that ministers put a high premium on the skills necessary to do well in it. Why? For one thing, management can often mean dealing with "it," with things; ministers want to deal with "thou," with people. They enter ministry in order to make a difference in the personal world. Many rebel against an overly technological, overly bureaucratized, supremely managed world. They want to stand at the side of people who need some creative schedule interrupting, some warm personal touches, and a chance to belong to something in today's world that is malleable, that ordinary people can change. They want congregations to be that, and they want their leadership to help protect them against the world of superefficient and often impersonal managers.

If a choice had to be made between the management world described in the first paragraph and the personal world described in the second, many readers of this book, and the writer of its foreword, would line up with the sentiments of the second. I, for one, have prejudices against books titled as this one is and against advertising topics such as the ones that these coauthors take up. Was humanity the subject of a covenant that it should all come down to efficiency? Was Israel led up out of Egypt so that one day we should be subject to the domain of credit cards, balancing

the books, and running meetings on time? Did Jesus die so that
managers might live? Are the royal priesthood, the holy nation,
the peculiar people of early Christian times succeeded by a royal
cohort of the managed? Keep the managers of the world at a distance, say the prophets and pastors of God's people—and with
good reason.

Yet, the coauthors are not interested in management that leaves
people out. They are disturbed that so many ministers pose themselves over against the right kind of management. They may be
even more disturbed over the fact that so many ministers have
not thought things through. Such ministers do not oppose management; they simply mismanage. They do not put a premium on
mismanagement. They just don't know how to administer or direct
complex organizations, such as local congregations.

Then, readers are going to find out, the people of God suffer.
They may not notice good management, but they will suffer from
bad operations. Laypeople who give of their time for each other
and the Lord through congregational life find that their donated
hours are wasted. They fritter away their time and expend emotions
in frustration. Bad management is bad stewardship, and laypeople
will feel it if their ministers do not know it on biblical grounds.
Why write this way and heap guilt on a sometimes burdened and
burned-out profession? But this is not the main point. I prefer to
see the issue from the Gospel side. Think how liberated one is
for the tasks of healing, counseling, consoling, preaching, and teaching if management comes to happen with ease and finesse.

I was tempted to say, "Think how well ministry will proceed
if there is first good management." *That* I cannot say after reading
this book. The authors are convincing—management is a form of
ministry. "Ad + ministry" or administration *is* ministry. It is not
behind the scenes, or preparation, or something to get out of the
way, or something to hide. It can be and is an expression of ministry
that is part of the whole healing, saving, judging, and enabling
process.

In forewords, it is bad manners to give away the plot and foolish
to waste readers' time repeating what they will soon read. It is
bad management, I guess we could say. A foreword should locate
a book. How did I overcome my suspicions of an often jargon-
filled field like management enough to read this manuscript? I
have known Samuel Southard's work for a long time and instinctively associated the word *pastoral* with it. It did not seem likely

that he would associate his name with anything manipulative, non-pastoral, or efficiently managerial at expense to people. And David S. Luecke started dropping in on me when he taught near by. He would leave manuscript chunks, ideas, and impressions. I became convinced that he had something distinctive to say.

The most fortunate feature of this book is the way the two play the roles they actually live and engage each other throughout. Where a reader feels a bit ill-at-ease because something is left out, a second author will soon come up with it and put it in. If that second author is vulnerable on some point or other, the first one represents the interests of the reader. Complementariness works in the readers' and users' favor.

The authors may not succeed in getting all ministers to stop worrying about and start loving management. They will, however, convince the open-minded and the ready that administration is central to ministry, that management can be a positive concept, and that ministers who manage well can minister well in more encompassing senses. This is a book full of thinking about management and ministry just as it is a book of "how to." I hope I have teased you into letting the two authors make their own case—which they do well.

MARTIN E. MARTY
The University of Chicago

1

Searching for an Integration of Management and Ministry

Administration, or management, is the most time-consuming work of pastors and the least satisfying to them. This "minister's dilemma" was pointed out several decades ago by sociologist Samuel Blizzard in a representative study of 690 ministers.

As these ministers told Blizzard about the various roles of their work, they tended to attach the most importance to their role as preacher, followed by pastor, priest, and teacher. Their roles as organizer and administrator were least important to them. Likewise, they felt most effective and satisfied in their preacher and pastor roles, with organizer and administrator again at the bottom of the list. Yet, it was these least preferred roles where they reported spending the most time.[1]

Dilemmas lead to stress. More recently, Edgar Mills and John Koval highlighted administration as a major source of stress for clergy. In their study of ministers in twenty-one denominations, they found that the ministers' stress was centered in professional duties rather than in family or other personal situations. Among the largest sources of occupational stress were conflict with members, overwork, financial or community troubles of the church, and staff problems.[2]

Why is there so much dissonance and stress between what pastors want to do and what they find themselves having to do?

One clue may come from Blizzard's conceptualization of the problem. He studied the dilemma in terms of the ways pastors tried to bring integration to their various functions. Most thought of themselves in terms that could be called a "father-shepherd." Additional popular self-images fit under "interpersonal relations specialist," "general practitioner," or "believer-saint." Only one in seven wanted to view himself as a "parish promoter"—seeing the church as something to be organized and seeing the minister as a leader of leaders in the organizational life of the church. For the others, organizational responsibilities seemed to remain mostly an intrusion on their real ministry.[3]

Images of ministry do change. Interviews today might bring out more themes along the lines of social concerns specialist, evangelist, healer, or church-grower. Yet, administration is still a side issue for many pastors. At least this is our impression, after years of interacting with pastors in continuing education seminars and of observing the many for whom discussions of church administration have little interest.

That churches do expect their pastor to provide administrative leadership for their organized efforts is clear. Ministers are too often inclined to approach such expectations as a set of duties that come with the job. Then administration seems mostly a matter of developing survival skills in the church, of learning how to cope better with the problems that arise as a pastor tries to get on with the real work of ministry.

If it remains just a way to solve unavoidable problems or to keep organizational wheels running smoothly, administration will continue to fall short of receiving serious attention by pastors. Our purpose in this book is to make the administrator role more appealing as a real ministry itself.

We are not going to do this by treating it as another specialty among the many others a pastor can pursue. This would only make the effort to integrate it all the more difficult. Nor do we propose to subsume all the other functions of ministry under administration, as if most pastors could learn to see themselves as chief executives in God's kingdom. This would be a hollow integration that runs counter to the motivation which brings so many men and women into ministry.

Rather, we intend to present management as an extension of

the ministry that pastors prefer to see themselves called to do. Our key concept is *pastoral administration*. There are many other kinds of administration, even in the church. They all share certain similarities and principles. But we will focus on administration the way a minister can do it as a pastor in a church as the body of Christ. "Pastoral" refers both to an office and to an attitude. The office is that of an overseer or a helmsman; and the attitude is Christlike caring that combines discipline and consolation in building up the body of Christ.

We presume to show how administration can become a source of pastoral joy, the sense of fulfillment in ministering that Jesus spoke of as his joy abiding in us. This joy is not the same as "fun," for it includes tasks that are often tedious and people who are frustrating. Pastoral joy—in any form of ministry—is a feeling that we have proven to do God's work in his body in a way that helps others and also gives us personal satisfaction.

For ministers with a sense of mission and a love for people, our appeal is to the personal satisfaction that can arise from making their administrative work serve fundamental ministry purposes. When it is integrated with the ministry they want to do, pastors can find joy in administration.

What the Complaints Suggest

At the core of most pastoral difficulty with the administrator role is a too-narrow view of the administrative function in the body of Christ. The part pastors are prone to recognize appears as an obstacle to the real ministry they want to do. As we shall see, the bias that a particular pastor has can often be anticipated.

We can tell something is incomplete by the kinds of complaints ministers often make about administration. Some want to focus on mission or programs and find themselves complaining about the difficulty of having to work through so many people to get things done. Others want to focus on relating to people and complain about the "busy work" distractions of keeping up with so many programs.

The first type comes in several forms. Ministers who want to invest energy in the tasks of church work are often dissatisfied because members are not active and cooperative in building up church programs. These pastors become impatient with the many demands of finding workers, developing agreements, and coordinating committees. Somehow, this does not seem to measure up in significance to the big mission they are trying to accomplish. Usually, these pastors are tempted to take on most of the administrative burden, great and small, so that their timetable for action will be met. When they cannot get help, the burden can become heavy indeed.

These pastors are like others who see administration as tasks to be done, but they differ in whom they see as responsible. The others expect someone else to do it. Acutely aware that many things should be done, they are accustomed to complaining about delays, sloppy procedures, and the lack of vision among their members. Often uninterested in the details, they lay heavy burdens on others but are slow to lift a hand to help. They then are disappointed by the lack of administrative success.

These complaints reveal a narrow view of administration. Whether they are successful or unsuccessful in this area, such pastors have a faulty concept of the function. They cannot really see how the church is built-up through the building up of people. Further, programs come first for them. They certainly would admit the importance of personal spiritual maturity in the congregation, but they cannot see how this could be related to organizational development. Personal growth is confined in their minds to individual acts of piety or participation in large meetings where the challenge is laid out for all to accept.

Another group of pastors looks primarily not at programs but at people. They see administrative tasks as a distraction from the supportive relationships they want to offer directly in their ministry. These pastors complain that many days they must sit in their office and shuffle papers when they should be out among their people. They are restless and depressed when questions about money or procedures press upon them. They openly say that all of these matters must be carried out by competent laypeople, while the pastors concentrate upon personal growth and facilitate group experience.

These pastors have missed the importance of an essential component in the growth of adults that was noted by psychiatrist Erik Erickson—the development of craftsmanship. Erickson presents craftsmanship as an essential ingredient of growth into adulthood, by which a person's identity is confirmed through the performance of a chosen task in society. When a young adult knows that he has done a good job in the accomplishment of a goal, which has been agreed on by him and his colleagues or the general public, his identity is firmly established and he has demonstrated an ability to contribute to society.[4]

Pastors who miss this essential aspect of adult growth are not only frustrated within their administrative task demands, but they also have attitudes that frustrate church officers. These officers wonder why the pastor cannot work with them in accomplishing the church's organizational goals. They also resent his preoccupation with people who have trouble and need counsel. In one elder's lament, "The only way I could get my pastor's attention was to be sick."

Pastors who prefer to see mostly the needs of the people in front of them are also likely to be ineffective at activating a church mission that reaches beyond the immediate concerns of the members. They may have high ideals for supportive outreach. But they fail to appreciate how much the routine functions of administration can become tangible expressions of love and justice. "The church is not relevant enough" is a charge that often accompanies such impatience with the role that is best suited to turn intentions into outcomes.

When we hear all of these complaints, what can we conclude? Really, there are two different understandings of administration that are inadequate. One puts too much emphasis on tasks or goals of a program without sufficient awareness that management is movement toward goals through people. The other places too exclusive attention upon the personal needs of congregation members without an awareness of the way in which designated responsibilities and the accomplishment of organizational goals contribute to the building up of individuals within the body of Christ.

A more comprehensive view of pastoral administration would include some elements from each of these extremes. We do not advocate the abandonment of either emphasis, upon task or upon people, but we do believe that both of these orientations toward the work of ministry can come together in an integrated concept of pastoral administration.

The Possibility of Integration

Is it possible to integrate administration and organization within the general framework of the pastoral role?

In previous research, David Luecke studied the professional perspective and the organizational perspective of fifty-six pastors. Under "professional," he included the emphasis they placed on conventional ministry functions such as preaching, teaching, and counseling. In comparison to these activities, the importance they attached to organizational and administrative functions in the church turned out to be a better predictor of their effectiveness as pastors.

The pastors who could combine a high interest in both perspectives—called synthesizers—were slightly more effective than those whose emphasis was mostly on organizational affairs. Where the synthesizers stood out, however, was in their personal satisfaction in ministry. They conveyed a strong sense of knowing what they were trying to do in their church and how they were going to get it done. Their self-reported satisfaction measured significantly higher than that of any of the other ministers with their one-sided emphasis or no strong emphasis at all.[5]

When James Ashbrook surveyed the administrative competence of more than one hundred pastors and asked over five hundred of their lay leaders for comments, he found the two extremes of task orientation and people orientation. But he also found successful pastors who could combine these emphases. The successful pastors were in churches with a high percentage of the budgets designated for benevolences, indicating a strong sense of morale fellowship in the congregation.

In Ashbrook's study, these ministers could tell *why* as well as *how*. They could relate specific programs to the congregation's general theological goals, explain the necessity for a particular effort at a particular time, and visualize the importance of various people in the activity. They expected and encouraged initiative on the part of members. There was freedom of expression and tolerance of differences.

At the same time, these ministers could handle the *how to*. There was a good sense of timing in their pastoral leadership, a talent for the breaking down of complex and abstract ideas into definable tasks that people could accomplish. Such pastors could describe actions in logical sequence and define how much was expected of various leaders to complete their part of some larger goal.

The *why* and *how* were one in such a pastor's awareness of people and programs. There was delight with the personal growth and independence of individuals, but there were also specific expectations of responsibilities within the total fellowship. Pastors in this integrated role could see the connection between faith and works, between people and programs.[6]

Your Personal Integration

By now, you may be partially persuaded that there is something to our argument for a more comprehensive view of pastoral administration. So far, we have based it on an appeal to your enlightened self-interest, when you cannot avoid work that too often seems to be an unwelcome appendage to your real ministry. We will add more arguments in subsequent chapters.

But if you are realistic, there are nagging questions in your mind. Can I achieve more integration, even if I wanted to? A second question is more basic. Will I want to change my attitude toward how administration fits into my ministry?

In partial answer to the first question, leadership studies suggest that you can improve your integration of task emphasis and supportive rational concerns.[7] But you should not imagine that there is an ideal type or style of leadership into which you should try to fit yourself. These two dimensions are the various ingredients of any leadership style, and experienced leaders do approach them differently. Effectiveness depends on recognizing what kind of leadership behavior is needed in specific, changing situations. Leaders who can shift their style as needed have an advantage. But those who remain comfortable with one dimension can still allow for and encourage the contribution of complementary leadership by others. Expanding your understanding of the dimensions will help make that possible, even if you are hesitant to change your personal leadership style. (See note 7 for research supporting these observations.)

Similarly, we are not going to advocate an ideal integrated ministry role into which you should try to fit yourself, especially against your own pastoral instincts. We ourselves cannot agree on what such a role would look like. Rather, we urge you to recognize your own ministry strength and seek to add to it. Perhaps, you can augment the emphasis you place on what you do personally. But integration can also happen by increasing your appreciation and encouragement for the complementary contribution of others with whom you work in the church. Our aim is to stretch your understanding of pastoral administration, starting with what comes naturally to you.

In answer to the second question, we think that the desire to change your attitude toward pastoral administration is not something you can achieve very well by yourself. Our experience is that pastors move toward greater integration through dialogue with others who see ministry and leadership differently than they do. Some pastors are blessed with colleagues and lay leaders who are respected enough, and irritating enough, to focus attention on aspects of their leadership that can be improved. Such encounters are not always pleasant.

It is more than happenstance that this book will be in a general dialogue format. But letting us talk to you, while we talk to each other, is no substitute for your own dialogue with those who know you and your work. We hope the possibilities we sketch out will help to make such dialogues of your own more attractive and constructive.

Ultimately, any willingness to change attitudes about ministry will flow from a more basic desire to be an effective servant of the Lord in ministry to his people. It is this commitment to serve that makes any stretching beyond personal preferences desirable. In a fundamental sense, the desire to find pastoral joy in administration depends on letting the call to ministry be heard in new ways.

Steps You Can Take Toward Integration

We suggest five steps you can take to move toward a larger view of pastoral administration that is more integrated with the rest of your ministry: (1) identify your natural emphasis; (2) understand the source of your dissatisfaction with administration; (3) recognize that the administrator role is bigger than you are; (4) be open to comprehensive leadership through mutual ministry; and (5) promote leadership dialogue about complementary contributions.

1. *Identify your natural emphasis.* Like other leaders, pastors have a natural tendency to emphasize either supportive relationships or structured tasks. Understanding this preference is the starting point.

The core value of the people orientation is consideration for the feelings of individuals, for their comfort and well-being. Such a leader wants to be fair in giving attention to all and is concerned about being easily approachable on any occasion. His or her pastoral instinct is to *comfort* people.

The dominant value in the task orientation is to see people in relation to a mission or a goal. The leaders with this emphasis want to think and talk about expectations for what people should do and how they can do it. Their pastoral instinct is to *challenge* people.

The best way to recognize which is your dominant value is to check yourself on how you react to ambiguous or stressful situations. When the pressure is on, the task-oriented pastor will react first to what is not getting done and will try to initiate or restore structure to the situation. The relationship-oriented pastor will react first to the feelings of the others involved and will try to put them at ease or help them feel better. One fears that someone will be offended. The other fears that something will not get done.

Both values may be equally present and strong in the pastor. But he or she may have achieved this through the experience of self-reminders to pay more attention to it. That which takes extra conscious thought probably does not come instinctively.

Here are some specific behaviors that are commonly associated with task-oriented or relationship-oriented leadership. As you look over each list, consider how typical of your leadership these are:

Some Task-Oriented Leadership Behaviors

- Planning the day's activities in detail
- Maintaining definite standards of performance
- Letting members know what is expected of them
- Being first in getting things done
- Emphasizing the meeting of deadlines
- Keeping the work moving at a rapid pace
- Asking members to follow organizational lines
- Seeing to it that the work of members is coordinated
- Being critical of poor work
- Seeing to it that staff members are working up to capacity

Some Support-Oriented Leadership Behaviors

- Putting suggestions of others into operation
- Looking out for the welfare of individual members
- Being friendly and approachable

- Discouraging individual criticism of group behavior
- Doing little things to make it pleasant to be a member
- Finding time to listen to other members
- Asking to be called by first name
- Getting approval on important matters before going ahead
- Engaging in friendly jokes and comments during meetings
- Not taking sides in cases of disagreement [8]

If you are still unsure of your natural tendency, ask people who know you. They are usually better evaluators of your actual leadership behavior than you are.

If you are really serious about identifying the inclinations in your leadership, several questionnaires are available for this purpose. One of the most popular is the LEAD-Self developed by Paul Hersey and Kenneth H. Blanchard (copyrighted by the Center for Leadership Studies).[9] Also popular is the self-assessment questionnaire used by Blake and Mouton in their "managerial grid." [10] Fred Fiedler suggests that your attitudes toward fellow workers are a good indicator of your dominant approach, and he offers a quick checkup on your "least preferred co-worker." [11]

Perhaps you are among those who emphasize both dimensions with equal strength. But if you are not, should you be afraid to admit that one is less evident in your ministry than the other? No. Your natural tendency and knowing the flock one by one is important for shepherding a congregation. Pastoring involves readiness to accept and affirm specific individuals as they are and to respond to their present needs. Also, leading a flock to their destination is being a good shepherd. Pastoring involves a readiness to see what people can do in their life together and to build up the church for the future.

2. *Understand the source of your dissatisfaction with administration.* We assume we are addressing pastors who have trouble finding church administration to be a source of real joy in their work. The next step is to understand where the dissatisfaction arises.

We suggest that pastors complain about administration when they view it as calling on them to do more of what does not come instinctively. They focus on the demands that take them away from their natural interests. The obstacles these pastors project depend on their preferred starting point.

For pastors who are oriented foremost to the feelings and

concerns of people, administration may look mostly like something that pulls them away from people rather than toward them. What they see represents demands that are a couple of steps removed from direct personal relationships—being sure procedures are established and followed, keeping records and making reports, talking about money, confronting people with difficult decisions. All of this gets in the way of a "personal" ministry. A people-oriented pastor is prone to focus on the task side of administration and feel, deep down, that these activities do not really serve people.

For pastors who react foremost to goal-directed tasks, administration may also seem like something that pulls them away from what they want to do, but for a different reason. What they often see represents hours and hours of relational demands that are only indirectly related to getting something done—being sure others feel confident about what they are supposed to do, adjusting to their ideas, keeping them enthused, recognizing their contributions. This investment of preparatory time seems like a distraction. A task-oriented pastor who dislikes administration is prone to focus on the support side of the administrative role and perhaps agree, in principle, that this work is necessary. But he or she experiences reluctance to divert that much of his or her effort into supporting the work of others.

For those who like to be supportive, such relationships can seem easier to maintain without constant reminders of things to be done; having to do administrative prodding makes it harder to be a friend. For pastors ready to get on with the next task, their work can seem a lot easier without the burden of carrying others along. Things they can do on their own, like preaching or teaching, have more attraction.

3. *Recognize that the administrator role is bigger than you are.* Why not concentrate on the dimension of administrative leadership that is a better fit for your own inclinations? This is ultimately what pastors do when they are able to turn administration into a fulfilling ministry. But there are a couple of steps in-between. Crucial is the recognition that, even in a church, overall administrative responsibility comes as a role bigger than the person who happens to be in it.

Underlying our approach is the assumption that administration really is a role. It is the performance of activities aimed at meeting the expectations of others. Much of the rest of ministry may not seem like such because the pastor has more latitude to act according to his or her personal expectations about what is important. Being a preacher, a teacher, or a friend can become largely what the pastor makes of it. It is more possible to fit these ministries to the person.

The person usually has to be fitted into the administrator role. Such leadership is a continual response to situations as seen by others, who develop rather clear impressions about what should be done and how they should be treated in the process. The fact that pastors report spending so much time doing administration, even when they dislike it, underscores the dominance of expectations other than their own.

Across the full range of church life, Christians are like other people who expect administrative help with accomplishing important shared goals as well as support of their individual efforts. How can we say that a leader usually leans toward either a task-oriented or a support-oriented response and then say that, as an administrator, a pastor has to be good at both?

We are not advocating that a pastor, like St. Paul, can be all things to all people. In fact, we want to say that few pastors can fulfill well all the leadership functions of the church at all times, even when they are trying to counterbalance their natural leaning. It is important to admit this limitation. The alternative is to try covering it up. Then pastors find themselves struggling on their own to redefine the role—or resenting that it is there at all.

The church is a wonderful place for admitting limitations. God loves his people as they are, and ministers do preach acceptance of one another. Usually, God's people can love and accept the pastor with his or her limitations, too. In their expectations for an administrator, what they really want is a minister who recognizes their need for both dimensions of administrative leadership. When a pastor admits a weakness in providing one or the other, church people are often quite willing to join in finding ways to compensate. What causes trouble is having that need ignored.

But why should a pastor admit such a leadership limitation? This question leads to a central theme of our writing. The character of an organized Christian fellowship calls for more than any one leader can usually accomplish alone. A Christian pastor is always dependent upon the body of Christ for the fulfillment of his ministry. In this, the pastorate differs from "professions" in which a highly trained and powerful person can be effective by individual efforts alone.

Why are church leadership requirements more complex than most individual leaders can meet? When we look into the New Testament for an answer, we find Paul's determination to do his ministry so that through the church the "many-faceted" wisdom of God will be made known to all (Eph. 3:9, 10). The New Testament describes the many facets of church life that are to reflect God's wisdom with themes like these: confronting with challenges while offering comfort; striving for independence while becoming more dependent; constituting one body, yet consisting of many individual parts; living in freedom, yet being a servant of all. The goal-task-structure dimension and the support-consideration-people dimension expressed in current leadership language are variations of these themes. One way or another, pastoral administration has to be done with respect for God's full wisdom for his people.

4. *Be open to comprehensive leadership through mutual ministry.* Getting all the leadership functions performed well is not the same as being good at all administrative functions. The latter statement stresses one person trying to be a star performer. The first opens up the possibility of several leaders sharing the role. We think this is the better way to find a more desirable ministry in church administration.

What we are advocating is a mutual ministry of church administration. Such shared leadership involves more than dividing up responsibilities, planning out different assignments, or delegating "authority." In the most basic sense, it can mean complementing each other's natural leaning. One leader who sees mostly tasks to be done and another who sees mostly feelings to be considered have a lot to offer each other, as well as the people they serve. They can tap that potential, so long as both understand the overall administrative function and appreciate what each brings to it.

To meet the challenge of a fully functioning body of Christ, leadership must be comprehensive rather than competitive. The pastor is not required to be or to do all that is needed in leadership. But the pastoral responsibility is to know and appreciate the importance of these varied functions. The ordained clergyman will fulfill some aspects of the role well. Other members will perform other aspects better. In it all, the pastor's high calling is to see that the needs of the body are met to the best of the ability of all who can contribute leadership.

5. *Promote leadership dialogue about complementary contributions.* Pastors who can admit the necessity of a mutual ministry are ready for the most practical step in integrating administration with their own ministry. That is to initiate and sustain dialogue with other leaders who react to situations differently. These may even be pastors of other congregations. But they could just as well be members of the pastor's own church.

We assume that most churches in fact do have gifted and experienced leaders other than the pastor. There are men and women who, in some capacity, are responsible for the welfare and productivity of others in work or social organizations. They may care deeply about the life of the church. They may also know better than the pastor the frustration and satisfaction of trying to help people feel good while trying to accomplish things together. The pastor certainly has something to teach them. But they will have something to teach the pastor, too.

The same men and women will undoubtedly be part of implementing the shared leadership that emerges. But we are addressing here the active step a pastor can take toward a fuller appreciation of the ministry of administration. The best way to move toward an effective and balanced perspective on pastoral administration is to learn from other committed Christian leaders whose leadership leanings are opposite to those of the pastor. The needs they are responding to are important to listen to.

This step means resisting the urge to talk frankly about administrative concerns only with people who share the same leadership values and ways of operating. This natural inclination is easy and comforting. It keeps perspectives narrow, however. Dialogue with people who think differently is hard work, but it can be very stimulating.

One pastor we know had his whole ministry changed through such dialogue with a layman in his congregation. Steve's partner, Charlie, was a businessman who operated an appliance store and knew a lot about management. Charlie was also president of the congregation. He had the courage to challenge the pastor about his overemphasis on relational ministry. Steve had the good sense to listen, even though their relationship was strained at times.

Finally, Steve learned to see the needs of the church in new ways. He became more willing to devote pastoral energy to task-oriented administration of carefully planned and coordinated programs. Together, Steve and Charlie developed congregational leadership involving a large number of members in a structured mutual ministry. Today, Steve is a seminary professor of church administration (at a seminary other than ours). He is a strong advocate of leadership dialogue.

Our Dialogue about Pastoral Administration

We think we can contribute to such dialogue through the writing that follows. After several years of teaching and talking together about church administration, we finally recognized that, indeed, we each have a different starting point for what we see and respond to. Even though many of our themes were common, we approached them differently. We discovered firsthand the value of balancing each other and the stimulation that comes in the process.

We can each talk about support and task, consideration and structure. We each regularly try to be comprehensive in our presentations on church administration. But Southard intuitively leans toward the support orientation, responding to people as he finds them to be and thinking about how to keep them together in common efforts. Luecke intuitively leans toward the task orientation, inquiring about goals and looking for ways to move people in shared activities.

We discovered that our dialogue really exists at two levels. There is the straightforward exchange that reminds each of the other necessary emphasis. This is the dialogue that will remain basic to most of our discussion of church administration.

This exchange has a support-oriented leader discussing the relational values that are most naturally dominant in his or her approach. Likewise, the task-oriented leader shares why goals and structures are so important. In effect, each assumes that the other's values are incomplete or misplaced. Each tries to entice the other to work harder at the dimension of administrative leadership that instinctively is less comfortable.

The second level of dialogue produces more insight and sets the stage for a more effective collaborative effort in the administrator role. For us, this happened when each realized that the other actually did appreciate and work with the opposite dimension. We just approached it differently.

In this sort of exchange, the person with one intuitive leaning discusses the dimension of administration that appeals most to the other. A support-oriented leader shares how he or she understands and approaches task accomplishment. A task-oriented leader talks about rationale and method for approaching relational ministry.

This dialogue assumes, of course, that each does recognize and understand both dimensions of administrative behavior. That is why it is a second-level dialogue.

We think we are at this level. Both of us have pastoral experience, although not comparable. We both have significant administrative experience in large organizations. Southard especially identifies with the counseling functions, which he teaches and does. He uses counseling models, vocabulary, and style. Luecke especially identifies with management functions, which he teaches and does. He uses management models, vocabulary, and style.

We each say some things that do not quite connect with the other. But we intersect at enough points to keep our dialogue interesting and productive for us. We have even reached the point where we do not feel defensive about our differences. This is when dialogue can be really constructive.

We offer our views as a second-level dialogue. It is our hope that you will find yourself attracted to one or the other starting points. We hope we can then make the other dimension more interesting for you.

Key Questions

If you are willing to enter this dialogue with us, you will be preparing for similar sharing with other church leaders. But the initial sharing will be difficult without some reference points, some way to organize the exchange among leaders about the basic functions of church administration. In the following chapters, we will pursue some questions about comprehensive leadership in the church that will help you in dialogue, first within yourself and then with your leaders.

In doing this, we believe that the right questions are essential for any building up of concepts about the administrator role in the church. This is a necessary step to organize thoughts in such a way that pastoral administration can be talked about in terms of people and tasks. If our basic assumptions are comprehensive—as revealed in our questions—then integration has a better chance of developing.

So, here are the six key questions that organize our dialogue in this book. They are for you to think about as you develop specific answers for your administration. And they are for your leaders to think about with you.

1. *What is the fundamental contribution of the pastor as an administrator?* Two different phrases focus on this contribution. Practicing *love with justice* underlies the people orientation of Southard. For the task emphasis of Luecke, the key is shaping the *covenant for a journey.* Both concentrate on the relationships of God's people sharing their common life. The pastor who first sees people as they are recognizes their hope for loving relationships and strives to reduce any inequities in the way they distribute and sustain their love. The pastor who sees people in terms of what they can do recognizes their need for a common understanding of their various contributions, and he strives to increase their trust in each other by fashioning agreements about where they will go and what they will do.

2. *Why is the administrator role so important in churches today?* We live in a complex, technological society in which organizations are necessary for stable and understandable relationships between people. The administrator role has risen in importance as the methodology of formal organizations has gained acceptance in modern churches. From a structural viewpoint, Luecke takes the organizational dimension of a congregation as a given in most churches. He describes the administrator role in terms of taming the organization to assure that it serves its intended purpose, which is kept in focus by staying clear about how the organization needs to justify its service to the church. Southard looks at the ethical aspirations of church members apart from an organization and sees diversity in expressions of love and justice. He describes the basic contribution that organizational forms make to the way Christians come together and live out Christlike qualities in their relationships with each other.

3. *What is the personal vision that can excite an administrator?* So much of administrative work becomes routine. What is it that can turn an administrator on and make the contribution exciting? Southard gains satisfaction from a counseling approach. He thinks of the psychodynamics of change in individuals and their ability to cope in interpersonal situations. So, he describes the satisfaction of helping to reconcile the strong and weak members. He sees the administrative challenge as keeping them working together on new relationships of love, despite the differing needs of independent and dependent personalities. Luecke is fulfilled by a structural approach in which organizations enhance the health and wholeness of people through social interactions. He draws on the image of building the body of Christ and looks to the satisfaction an administrator can have when serving as an architect of the relationships that join Christians together in their fellowship and mission.

4. *How can administrators "move" people?* So much of the ministry revolves around moving people as individuals toward growth in their personal faith and Christian living. The administrator role adds to this the stimulation and guidance of such movement as it becomes a shared and coordinated response of many individuals. The underlying question is how to influence the behavior of people with different personal agendas. Southard recognizes influence for what it is—power. He sees it as an attribute that many, besides the pastor, bring with them into their church life. He offers counsel on how to affirm their power, build up the church body through the power of the people, and keep them working together with the pastor. Luecke steps back from direct relationships and focuses on arranging the contexts in which people will move themselves to act in ways that satisfy their own needs while meeting program objectives. He takes a management view of motivation and recommends the selection and training emphases of personnel management.

5. *How should administrators handle conflict?* Conflict is a disturbing and distracting intrusion in the work of ministry done in the traditional roles, when the interaction between support and task is not well appreciated. Administratively, we see conflict as both a problem and an opportunity for personal understanding

and enriched interaction. Southard describes how support-oriented administrators can stimulate a search for the suggestions and actions that help participants to cope with changes in their life together and to work out accommodations of their differences. Luecke explores when administrators should address conflict. The key administrative issue is when to be helpful by reducing conflict before it occurs and when conflict would be better left to resolve after relationship difficulties emerge.

6. *How can administrators contribute to good communication?* Effective administrators find themselves bringing special emphasis into their communication with members whose actions they are trying to guide. Luecke concentrates on showing how a church has a variety of message sources that can be exchanged between members. Administrators should strive to broaden and strengthen the range of sources intentionally used. Southard shows how the range of communication should be balanced with pastoral specificity and support and how the specialized language of administrators can do this.

Getting Specific

As reflected in these questions, we seek to probe attitudes and to aid in the development of concepts. Good theology and theory go a long way toward making necessary work more interesting—and effective.

This approach runs the risk of losing contact with administration as pastors most often see it—a constant flow of specific situations and people that need attention. The best way we know to bring the general and the specific together is through the use of cases. Thus, each chapter begins with a specific, realistic church situation that calls for a pastor's response. We have addressed the general questions with answers that speak to the immediate need of the case at hand. Aside from making the reading more interesting, we hope this approach provides a model for the personal dialogues we are encouraging between pastors and other leaders. To come together on the generalities, start with the specifics.

We realize that we will not answer many of the "how to" questions that arise in day-to-day administration of a church, such as how to make up a budget, how to manage facilities, or how to plan special events. We believe suitable texts are available on these subjects, and we recommend a variety of them at the end of this book. Our purposes are accomplished if a pastor discovers an increased motivation to search out those specific answers.

2

The Pastoral Contribution through Administration

Mrs. Frye's Gift

"A gift of $50,000 would be almost a third of the church budget!" thought Pastor Westin. Then the joy of the gift from Mrs. Frye was tempered by the thought, "Where will it do the most good?" With an inner jolt, the pastor realized that a dozen people had told him "what's good for the church," and each idea was different. How could this gift express the "common" good? Who knew what was most needed now and in the future for the church? Could a group come to a consensus without some disappointment and the cry of "Unfair! Our needs were ignored"?

Pastor Westin felt that he must find some answers, for Mrs. Frye had just called to say, "I don't know if I should designate this gift or not. What is your advice, Pastor?" Now the fifty-year-old pastor confessed to himself that he didn't have this kind of wisdom. What to do? Then he remembered an Old Testament verse, "In the multitude of counselors there is safety" (Prov. 11:14, NKJV). He sat down and wrote out a list of the "natural" church leaders—some in office and some not—who knew the needs of the church and would be listened to in any discussion of the $50,000.

After a prayer for wisdom, the pastor began his list: the chairmen of finance, deacons, members of the planning committee, plus a relative of Mrs. Frye who was the most wealthy and generous member of the congregation. As the pastor stared at the list, he recognized a glaring error—no women. But then he thought that Mrs. Frye always listened to men so he didn't add a woman to the list.

Then he called Mrs. Frye and read the list to her. She agreed to meet with these men in the pastor's home for informal counsel.

When the informal counselors met, there seemed to be an unspoken feeling that each person should subordinate his own needs to the greatest good of the church. Pastor Westin was impressed that the men who had spoken with great certainty to him about the needs of the church were now speaking moderately about a particular proposal and listening carefully to other proposals.

This spirit was the only consensus of the meeting, except for a common acknowledgment that the gift should not be designated. No three people in the pastor's living room could agree on exactly how the $50,000 should be spent. But, at least, there was a nodding of heads to the pastor's summary:

> It seems that several needs came up most often in our discussion. We need educational space, especially for the children. We need a gym, or something like it, for the youth. There's a strong yearning from some middle-aged members for an organ. So, if I've sensed the needs [nodding], I'll convene the church council, which several of you are on this year, and begin formal discussion of the need or needs that would be met through this gift. The council represents all ages from youth up and most of our key committee chairpersons. Will it be representative? [Nodding.] Then we'll do it. Now, let's pray. If some of you feel led, pray, and I'll close.

SOUTHARD

To Practice Love with Justice

Whether or not he wants to be, Pastor Westin is an administrator. In reacting to Mrs. Frye's offer of the $50,000 gift, he cannot avoid the role. She is looking to him for leadership. The church leaders are looking to him for leadership. Pastoral generalities will not be enough. The money is real, and the expectations of what to do with it will be specific. He has to layout some course of action that others can follow.

As a pastoral administrator, what can Pastor Westin contribute to this situation? He could see this as an opportunity to pursue his own agenda for the church. If he were simply to announce his personal preference for an organ, a building addition, or whatever, Mrs. Frye might well agree, and the matter would be settled. This would be one type of leadership. But it would not be good church administration. He would miss the opportunity to make a pastoral contribution much more significant than just getting some project funded.

In his administrator role, Pastor Westin can help give concrete meaning to the Christian love this church as a body wants to practice in their relationships with each other. How this congregation practices love in reacting to this gift will demonstrate what they are about.

What kind of love are we talking about? Is it only applicable to individuals, like Mrs. Frye? Or is it the cozy feeling we have with people who agree with our own views and enhance our self-esteem?

No. The love that is the basis of church life is love that is practiced with justice. The exercise of justice means that the needs and interests of others are taken into account in decisions about individual acts that could affect them. Conditioning love with justice is most necessary when needs are in conflict.

Pastor Westin has a good start on demonstrating the practice of love with justice in this situation. He recognized the objective when he noted that "there seemed to be an unspoken feeling that each person should subordinate individual needs to the greatest good of the church." At the same time, he did not wish to ignore personal needs, for he closed the meeting with references to the church council in which people of all ages would be represented. Also, he accepted very strong opinions from the different people who were meeting with Mrs. Frye.

I affirm this pastor's approach to church administration. He is trying to see individuals in the congregation as they are, to recognize their hope for loving relationships. He also sees them as a group and hopes to reduce the inequities in the way by which they distribute the goods and services of the church and try to sustain mutual love.

Administration is the ministry of shaping the practice of this kind of love through a Christian community. Three theological principles undergird the significance of this contribution:

1. The longing for love must be shaped by the doctrine of the Trinity and Christ's sacrifice.

2. The exercise of justice is to sustain the practice of love.

3. The power to increase love with justice is a function of the body of Christ as guided by the Holy Spirit.

Sacrificial Love as the Basis of Fellowship

The beginning of a loving fellowship is the doctrine of God in three persons. This is the formation of fellowship within the Godhead. The love that flows from this fellowship is perfect obedience and mutual commitment (Phil. 2:5–11).

There are two aspects of this doctrine that give assurance to Pastor Westin as he seeks pastoral wisdom through a multitude of counselors.

One assurance is the belief that each person is created in the image of the fellowship of God (Gen. 1:26). We are created with the capacity to serve God on earth in fellowship with love. Therefore, when Pastor Westin calls a council meeting to discuss a question of love and justice, he knows this is the way that people have been created—to solve questions of love and justice in God's kingdom. He does not start with the assumption that he has all the answers himself or that he can look to one or two chosen counselors for all of the advice he needs. Such an action would be a contradiction of trinitarian doctrine. God's plan for all work in the world is "the fullness of him who fills all in all" (Eph. 1:23), a phrase that translates today as "interdependent," reciprocal respect in decision making.

Also, Pastor Westin is secure in the knowledge that trinitarian doctrine requires a balance of individual and corporate needs in the discussion of Mrs. Frye's gift. It is clear from the creation stories (Gen. 2:5, 9–10; 4:10) that two questions come out of our creation as a people made in God's image. The first is: Who am I? The second is: Who is my neighbor? These are the two questions that lie behind the grouping of the church council and the meeting of an impromptu group to discuss a gift. Each person is to speak for personal interest or those of a representative group in the church or the community. If each person does not speak with reality and authenticity about identified needs, then the church is not well served in its planning for justice. Alongside this personal identity, there must be an awareness of the needs of others, a sense of neighborliness that, as Pastor Westin observed, caused each person to "speak moderately about a particular proposal and listen carefully to other proposals."

By acting as an administrator, Pastor Westin has provided an opportunity for various needs to be expressed. Both he and the lay leaders are more likely to act justly because of this informal discussion about ways to provide for the common good.

But more is required than a voicing of opinions. There must be a spiritual quality in the deliberations, a willingness to speak moderately and listen openly to others. This will require some sacrifice of ego and personal gratification. Why should Pastor Westin expect such moderation from business and professional people who are encouraged by the world to seek their own fulfillment? The answer is in the doctrine of Christ's sacrifice. It is his love for others that is both the model and the motivation for our relationships with one another and for our understanding of ourselves. We love because he first loved us and gave himself for us (1 John 4:11, 19).

Unless the men who meet with Mrs. Frye have been filled abundantly with this love, they cannot share it with one another. They will fight for that which seems "right" in their own eyes and feel personally deprived when Mrs. Frye's money goes to other purposes. Therefore, before a church leader can share God's love with others, he or she must first experience God's love. Once we are filled, then we can have fellowship. Those who receive the benefit of sacrificial love are willing to direct that love toward others (Eph. 2:11–22; Matt. 25:31–48).

This sharing of love must begin with the senior administrator of the church. In this case, it is Pastor Westin. If he feels enough of God's love in himself to share it with others, then he will be comfortable with their opinions and look for justice that incorporates the needs of many people, including himself. He will not press for his own opinion because he does not feel deprived of love.

How do we express these qualities of life that are based on God's image and Christ's sacrifice? It is in our responsible deliberations and our group decision making that we can both learn and practice these doctrines. Church management is an opportunity to do theology in the life of the church. Without these controlled and purposeful meetings, people may never learn the applications of Christ's life to their own life among fellow citizens and saints in God's kingdom.

What are some applications?

1. To be fully human is to be in fellowship with God and neighbor (Gal. 5:13–15; Eph. 4:17–32). If we live as we were originally created, we will expect and participate in the sharing of love as the original state of humankind. Fellowship and group decision making will be the most natural part of our life recreated in God's image.

2. Each person has a responsibility to contribute to fellowship (1 Cor. 14:26; Col. 3:12–17). God held Cain responsible for his false answer to the question: Where is your brother? This same sense of responsibility is presented again in Jesus' story of the Good Samaritan as an answer to the question: Who is my neighbor? Each person who affirms Christ as Savior must submit to Christ's lordship in the sharing of personal talents for the common good.

This principle may be illustrated in a later event from the case of Mrs. Frye's gift. The story is one I happen to know. The council voted to commit the gift to a building addition and program for a Christian Life Center. Soon after the decision, Pastor Westin met for lunch with two of the men who had originally met with Mrs. Frye. One of them was displeased with the way the money would be spent and didn't want to serve on a committee that would oversee the operation of the Christian Life Center. But the other man, who had called them together for lunch, exhorted him to stay with his original commitment. He began to see that he would not be accepted as a responsible leader in the congregation if he drew back from a project that he had helped plan.

3. The contribution of self to others is sacrificial (Rom. 5:1–11; Luke 10:25–37). This lesson was crucial to the member of the informal planning committee who wished to withdraw. In his eyes, he would have to sacrifice professional integrity to continue support of the Christian Life Center. As a local real-estate developer, he had always maintained a high percentage of his budget for maintenance of property. Over his arguments, this budget item had been cut from the operational expenses for the Christian Life

Center so that a part-time director could be employed for the center. How could a businessman who knew the importance of maintenance give his assent to a program in which this was ignored?

4. A new being and a self-giving being are only possible by recreation of the self in Christ's image (Phil. 2:1–11). As Pastor Westin thought about the people who were on his planning committee, he realized that all of them had inadequacies that would tempt them to get what they could from Mrs. Frye's contribution and be defensive against the requirements of others. How could they have the adequacy of self-giving people without the new sense of a redeemed self through Christ? Also, the pastor soon became aware that one or more members were tempted by their own adequacy, professional or otherwise, to limit commitment and fellowship to a program that everyone had developed together. Unless there was some continual recreation of the self in Christ's image, the sacrificial fellowship could not be maintained. Constancy of administrative oversight brought this to the attention of each person who felt a responsibility for the development of the center.

Justice and Power to Sustain Love

In the Book of Acts, it is clear that the early church faced some of the questions about its members that Pastor Westin faced about his planning committee. In both churches, there were people who were tempted to partial commitment, to party spirit, to pride, to envy, to defensiveness, and to lack of faith.

What is a church leader to do when these signs of sin are manifest? Sometimes, the response is blind sentimentality, in which leaders refuse to pay attention to the obvious signs of selfishness and unfaithfulness.

Another response is to say that, unless people can completely love each other in the spirit of Christ, no decisions can be made about their work together. When signs of sin continue to be manifest, the discouraged leadership will give up on programs and decide that the church can no longer be an organism, it can only be an informal gathering of people who are sentimentally attached to each other. Then the sentiment of warm creature feelings would never be threatened in the future with any challenge to make lasting and definitive decisions for the entire group.

A third possibility is to adopt the theological position that sin is a continuing reality in Christian as well as non-Christian organizations and that the remedy for sin is the exercise of justice. This is possible when just administration distributes loving service.

An alert reader will immediately think: "But what about repentance? Isn't this the answer to sin rather than 'justice'?" The reader is correct, if we think of repentance as a broken and contrite heart in the awareness of known sin.

But some people do not repent. This is especially true when we think of "unwitting sin," which means an unthinking transgression of the ritual law in the Old Testament. This can be translated under the New Covenant to mean the unchallenged assumptions of people who think that they are acting in a godly way.

In the context of church administration, justice deals both with the need for repentance in the case of known sin (Acts 5:1–11) and the unwitting sin of selective inattention (Acts 6:1).

Love is the basic motivation for repentance in all types of sin. But when the sin is found in the church, even as in the community and the society, power is necessary to make some people aware of their sin and to protect others against those who are unwitting sinners (Acts 5:11–12). Justice is the power that sustains love despite selfishness in the church and the community.

The function of just power is two-fold: (1) to distribute to all that which is due each person as a human being (common justice) and (2) to distribute to each according to talent, character, or circumstance of life (distributive justice).

The first use of just power is seen in Peter's challenge to Ananias and Sapphira. Each person who followed the example of Barnabas would sell land and bring the proceeds of the sale to the apostles. The honor and approval of the Christian community was the just reward for each person who did this, irrespective of the amount of money that was brought.

But Ananias and Sapphira were convinced that greater honor came to those who brought the largest amounts. Since they did not want all of their money to go to the church, they kept back part by deceit and were condemned. Why? Because they had subverted the principle of common justice. They wanted special recognition for partial payment.

Does this mean that all people in the church and in society are always to receive the same rewards for everything? In one way, the answer is yes. The pastor in the case of Mrs. Frye's gift was anxious that each group in the church should have equal representation in planning for the distribution of the money. It would not have been just for him to appoint only those of social rank and wealth to plan for the common good of the church. Also, the people who served on the planning committee sought to make a decision that would be of benefit to as many members of the congregation as possible.

In church law, this sense of just distribution to all is formulated in policies such as the right of all members of the congregation to vote on the annual budget or to call a pastor.

But alongside this function of justice, there is the distribution of power and services according to an individual's talent and the requirements of the office in which the individual will serve. This is demonstrated in the sixth chapter of Acts when the apostles declared that they should not leave God's word to serve tables. They have a specific function to perform as those who were face to face with Jesus in his earthly ministry; and because of their special relation to Christ, they receive honor above others. This honor does not mean that they are more Christian than anyone else. One of those who is called to serve at table, Stephen, is irresistible in his wisdom and spirit (Acts 6:10). But Stephen's function in the early church was different from that of the apostles. He did not have the close fellowship with Jesus that was accorded to the twelve and was, therefore, ranked initially among those who received recognition as one who was just below the apostles, but not one of them.

In church administration, problems can arise when these two functions of justice are confused. Suppose that a friend of Mrs. Frye were indignant because she was not chosen initially to meet for a discussion in the pastor's living room. What would the pastor reply? He might say: "You are right. A woman should have been represented in that initial meeting because the majority of the church members are women and the needs of all the congregation must be represented in any meeting that is called for the common good." But he also could have said:

This was a more specialized group to assist Mrs. Frye in the initial decision concerning the way in which the money was to be given to the church. Was it to be a designated gift, or was it to be a part of the general fund? Because this was a specialized question, I brought in the people who were considered by Mrs. Frye to be most knowledgeable about this particular question. Now that the question has been decided, we must be careful to see that the distribution of this money is made without regard to sex, age, or race. We will seek to provide this kind of justice through the appointment of a representative group that includes women.

I would hope that Mrs. Frye's friend would be satisfied, but I must admit that "distributive justice" was a chronic problem in my pastorates. For one thing, people often confused distributive justice with justice as access to decision making, goods, and services for all people in the church. This "common" justice is often confused with distributive justice because of the democratic ideal of most American churches. It often seems best to us that everyone should have a chance to take part in every decision and that all receive honor without distinction.

In a later chapter, I will talk more about the place of power in church life. This will be an opportunity to see how common and distributive justice are combined. For the present, my concern is to show that power is necessary to sustain love through justice and that this power must sometimes be concentrated in a group of people who have a specialized function, and, at other times, it should reside in the entire body of Christ.

Power in the Spirit

Whichever distribution of power we need at a particular time, there can be only one source of power to increase love in the body of Christ. This is the Holy Spirit. A pastoral administrator has to depend on the Holy Spirit to show how love with justice can be expressed in church life. What do we know from biblical theology about the way in which the power of the Spirit operates?

First, the Holy Spirit is our guide to an awareness of God's original purpose for his creation and to an openness to his order despite our resistance. This is one of the most prominent acts of the Spirit in the Book of Acts. Simon Peter's introductory sermon on the day of Pentecost is a detailing of evidence from Israel's history concerning God's original purpose for his people and his plan for their salvation through his Son. Christ is the new order of humanity who will replace the confused thinking and disorder of the people who live by their own works rather than by faith.

After that Pentecost experience, the original order of creation is particularly dramatized in the new community's selling of possessions to meet common needs, in the daily eating together, and in the mutual instruction and praise (Acts 2:44–47). These actions were evidence of the power of the Spirit through the apostles (Acts 2:43).

We show our own awareness of the original creation through an imitation of the Spirit and Spirit-generated interactions of fellowship that were found in the early church (even though we have little specific guidance concerning any organizational patterns in that church). The special contribution of church administration is to help guide the development of habitual patterns of relationships that channel love in accordance with Christ's life.

I graphically realized my dependence on the Spirit when, in one church, I proposed that women should serve as elders or deacons. I pointed to the respect with which Jesus spoke to and listened to women, according to the gospel record, and I noted Paul's proclamation that, in Christ, there is neither male nor female. I needed the specific guidance of the historical record of Jesus' life to counteract the cultural biases of a congregation in which women expressed their opinions through their husbands who were elected to office. This allowed the women to have power without responsibility, and the more traditional people liked it this way.

But there was not enough power of the Spirit in my recommendations. I did not really recognize the depths of cultural resistance, and I did not pray enough with and for the people in this decision. I was jolted into a dependence upon the Spirit's power when I realized that the people would bend to my wishes by placing women in nomination, but they would then elect men of new faith and immature personality rather than women of spiritual maturity and tested leadership in the community.

This defeat opened me to a better understanding of God's original order. The Spirit can create new patterns of interaction to replace channels that are becoming ineffective or to meet the needs of a changing society. But change in the body often happens slowly when the fellowship deliberates together. Church structure expresses the needs of God's people, and it changes only as they become sure, in the Spirit, of God's purposes.

The administrative problem is to know when new or old structures are adequate channels for love and when they are nothing more than the secure ways for church leaders to maintain their position. This distinction was important in my work with a committee at a church that was discussing the organization of Sunday school classes. Should they continue to have one large class for men and another for women? This structure was strongly defended by one of the traditionally minded women, who spoke as the president of the Women's Missionary Alliance. Or should the classes be restructured to let husbands and wives study the Bible together? This was strongly advocated by a younger woman, representative of younger couples who had started attending.

What is a pastor to do when such a confrontation occurs? If he or she is primarily concerned for personal security and status, deference will be paid to the traditional wisdom of the women's organization, and the younger woman will be placated for the time being. In contrast, a pastor might speak openly about change to both women. This is what I chose to do. I tried to show respect for both positions. But I tried to focus attention on the needs of the different age groups and the shifts in interest that were occurring in the congregation. I was able to clarify some issues for deliberation, which did bring some changes.

In the process, I found myself embodying two more functions of the Spirit in the body of Christ. One is to comfort and the other is to challenge. On the one hand, Jesus refers to the Holy Ghost as "the Comforter" (John 14:26). On the other hand, he refers to "the Spirit of Truth" who will not be received by the world (John 14:17).

Pastoral administration can provide comfort and challenge for all groups, whether they are traditional or change oriented. More of this will be presented in chapter 3. I continued to respect the traditionally oriented woman, sought her advice on many occasions, ministered to her and her family in time of illness, and rejoiced when she was elected teacher of the women's Bible class. I did not cut her off because I challenged her, and I hoped that my comfort to her was not seen by others as a compromise of the challenge to change.

What I depended on, both in comfort and in challenge, was the character of the individual Christians on the church council. Whether they were traditional or change oriented, men or women, old or young, I continually looked for the fruit of God's Spirit in their lives. Without this, we were not only powerless to plan in accordance with godly purposes for our congregation, we could not even go through the process of planning itself. I was fortunate to have leaders in every church who had this power of the Spirit in them.

Whatever choices are to be made in a church council, there must always be an awareness that the power for a Christian decision must reside in the Spirit of Christ rather than in institutional forms of management. These forms are of functional significance as routine channels of interaction between people who seek to serve Christ. But because the church's foundation is the service of Christ, it is his Spirit that mandates comfort or challenge, change or steadfastness. If a church leader desires the abiding power of the Spirit in a congregation, there must always be a question in every council meeting: In what ways do the structures of this church and the assumptions of our thinking inhibit or enhance spiritual power to practice love together?

Luecke

To Shape the Covenant for a Journey

Mrs. Frye's $50,000 gift is a wonderful blessing for God's people in this congregation. How often church leaders pray for such a "financial angel"! But let's face it. Pastor Westin now has a problem. Many ministers might well hesitate to trade places with him. Decisions have to be made, and they are not going to be easy.

Problem solving and decision making are basic to the contribution administrators bring to church life. Of course, everyone faces the need to deal with problems and make decisions. Administration as a distinct activity rises in importance when the problems involve more than a few people and the decisions affect many. The dozens and hundreds of people involved in the shared life and efforts of a Christian congregation can produce very complicated situations. Helping good things emerge out of them is a real ministry for pastoral leadership.

Resources, Needs, and Goals

Pastor Westin faces such a complicated situation. He can approach it two ways. One is to concentrate on assuring that injustices do not occur—that someone is not offended or some needs are not overlooked. This is the way emphasized by Southard, with his instinctive concentration on the support functions of leadership. Administration expresses love for each member by striving for a decision-making process that provides a fair hearing for all needs and interests. Such justice reduces the potential for a destructive outcome in this Christian community.

The other way is to concentrate on assuring that this congregation moves as far as it can toward achieving its full potential as God's people jointly expressing his will. This way looks at these people not only as they are now, but it especially sees them as they can be. Additional resources mean more than a distribution problem. They present the opportunity for this church to become something different in the future through some positive and exciting additions to their shared ministry. Helping this happen is the task orientation to which I instinctively respond.

To speak of tasks raises the question of goals. While Christian life has to start with being—being in Christ and being in fellowship with other believers—it quickly moves to doing—doing acts of response to God's call to each and all. In Christ, the doing is for a purpose. God's past actions give his people a future. Our actions lay claim on that future. The language of goals is our culture's way of speaking about the intentions for the future that guide the tasks we do today.

In the complicated situation facing Pastor Westin, he and the congregation have to make a decision about the $50,000 gift from Mrs. Frye. They have a new resource for ministry. Part of the administrator reaction is to look for needs. This was the first topic of discussion in the informal meeting of leaders. The next topic ought to be goals. A task-oriented Pastor Westin would work to keep the question of goals high on the agenda for deliberations about this gift. "What are we trying to accomplish here at Trinity Church?" he might ask more than once. As pastor, he might well have some ideas to contribute.

Resources. Needs. Goals. These three concepts form the context for administration. Whether in the church or any organization, administrators busy themselves with channeling shared resources to address specific needs in ways that accomplish agreed-upon goals. Facilitating a constructive linkage between the three concepts is the fundamental contribution administrators make.

Support-oriented leaders, like Southard, tend to emphasize the needs of those who are involved. Task-oriented leaders, like me, tend to concentrate on the goals for what they could do together. When the needs and goals are looked after within the constraints of available resources, we are talking about exercising the role of administrative leadership.

Table Serving and the Covenant

Stephen was the first church administrator. We read about his ministry in Acts 6 and 7. Actually, he was part of an administrative team made up of the seven "of good repute, full of the Spirit and of wisdom" chosen by the apostles. But it is Stephen we know best. He apparently was the leader of the team.

The initial description of these administrators may help account for the ambivalence pastors have felt about this ministry over the ages. They were appointed to distribute food to the widows of their community.

Now waiting on tables is certainly an honorable vocation. Many Christians do it for a living today. Undoubtedly, many pastors have done it at some time in their youthful days. If so, though, they probably did it with an eye toward leaving that phase of their life behind as they moved on to more "worthwhile" service, like the preaching the apostles did.

Often pastors look at church administration as something on the par with serving tables, necessary yet preferably left to others. The function needs an apology. What it contributes has to be explained and defended.

Stephen's ministry provides a wonderful vehicle to make that apology. To begin with, Stephen was the first martyr of the church. Whatever he was doing, it was a powerful witness to the claims God makes upon his people in Christ. More than the preaching of the apostles, his ministry of action pressed the limits of the tolerance of the religious establishment of the time. The priests reacted by encouraging and condoning his stoning. Church administrators today can sometimes feel a special kinship with Stephen and his painful death. They often feel like martyrs as they try to take action on complicated situations that arise in church life. Pastor Westin may well wonder whether he could experience martyrdom at Trinity Church.

Stephen's most evident contribution, short of his final witness, was the care of the widows. He and his team got "the daily distribution" where it was supposed to go. The most powerless members of the community were defended. Women and families who otherwise had trouble sustaining themselves were spared the indignity of begging. Justice was done in an elementary way.

Clearly, this administrative team was practicing love with justice. Stephen is an example of the support-oriented management emphasized by Southard. But I can see more in this administrative contribution than looking after the justice of providing for the meals. Reading between the lines, we can surmise that Stephen and his colleagues made a very significant contribution to forging and preserving the covenant base for the newly formed Christian community.

In those early days, the believers in Jerusalem were forming the everyday agreements and relationships that gave meaning to their shared life in Christ. They were becoming a covenant community. In Acts 2 and 4, we learn how they spontaneously responded to the call to follow Christ by pooling their wealth and resources for the common good. They had a fellowship that extended their sharing to everything they had, physical as well as spiritual. But what seems easy in a rush of enthusiasm, filled with the Spirit, often becomes more difficult as time goes by. The realities of new interests and competing claims on time and energy can whittle away at commitments. Sharing goes two ways, giving and receiving. What is a commitment made by one person becomes an expectation held by another. When expectations are disappointed, doubt and suspicion are not far behind. Without clearly understood agreements tested by time and practice, even a Spirit-led fellowship can deteriorate.

The murmuring of the Hellenists about their widows was the first serious test of the new community called together through the apostles' preaching. Earlier, Ananias and Sapphira, with their lies, tested the trust level. But they were individuals and could be dealt with face to face. The plight of the widows involved the disappointment of many people in scattered homes, and there was no quick fix. Did the community really mean what they professed about their commitment to each other? Was this just a fellowship of words, or would it become a covenant of reliable action?

Administrators concentrate on turning intentions into action in complicated situations involving a number of people. They do this by developing specific agreements among participants about the recurring pattern of relationships, about the structure that will guide their shared interaction over time. They nail down the commitments and expectations that give dependable substance to covenant hopes. Supporting individuals as they try to follow through on their commitment is part of the job. But shaping the structure that guides the relationships remains basic.

That the widow of Pronorus on Fourth Street got her food every day may not seem like much. Yet, Stephen and his fellow administrators may well have been central figures in preserving the vitality of that early church in which we are all rooted. At stake was whether Hebrew-speaking and Greek-speaking Christians could really live together in fellowship. For the Hellenists, the time came when actions spoke louder than words. Had their widows been slighted much longer, that fellowship may have divided, with who knows what consequences. The table-serving administrators strengthened the covenant and made it work.

The Covenant and the Journey

Shaping the covenant could be an administrative goal unto itself. Support-oriented leaders might settle for this. But the covenant of a church community should be seen as a means to a larger end. These future-oriented goals give the covenant its fullest meaning.

Stephen was definitely oriented to the future. While he did not speak modern goal language, he did concentrate on movement with a purpose. He was anxious to see the covenant people stay on a journey of discovering what God had in store for them. The task of moving on to new things was important.

We pick up these themes from his sermon in Acts 7. His actions and the testimony that went with them brought him before the council of Jewish leaders. Stephen was accused of supporting the effort of the followers of Jesus of Nazareth to change the customs of the existing covenant. It was his moment of truth. He responded with the longest sermon recorded in the Book of Acts. This was from a man appointed to be a food administrator by others who wanted to do the preaching.

Stephen's message is all about God's covenant people "on the way." In Genesis, the Lord initially made his covenant after Abraham responded to his call to go "to the land that I will show you." It was a covenant of the promise of increasing numbers of his children for obediently serving their Lord. But first, the chosen people had to be tested and moved to Egypt, then out into the wilderness, and on into the promised land. But even there, they were to be a people of the tabernacle, ready to move on as God led them. Stephen's point was that trouble began when God's people built a temple and thought the Most High would confine himself to a house made by hands. Trying to confine themselves to celebrating what they had made in the past and ignoring prophetic calls to the future, the covenant people resisted the Holy Spirit. There were new ways to go for those who stayed open to God's ongoing call through the Righteous One, the Christ. Stephen's work and words were a witness to the future that God held forth for his people.

These themes carry over to Pastor Westin and Trinity Church. God's people in their covenant congregations today are still being tested for their faithful obedience. They are still being called to stay on the move to avoid getting comfortable with what they made in the past. The Holy Spirit is still at work creating new possibilities. Church life remains a shared journey following the Lord's lead.

It is only through God's word that we can keep the vision of the journey alive among God's people today. The ministry of the Word comes first and foremost. The apostle's instincts were right when they chose to manage their time so they were not distracted from prayer and preaching. Yet, the journey does not get underway until the vision starts turning into a reality. Stephen's ministry of administration is a reminder that the ministries of serving and doing make this happen.

Significantly, Stephen's sermon is about men of action—most of whom we today would recognize as administrators. He speaks well of Joseph (another administrator of food, among other things) and Moses (who used his organizing skills to give structure to the Israelites for their most important journey). King David, a gifted administrator, continued the quest for the future of God's people. But the covenant shifted with the administration of King Solomon, who ended the quest in the building of the temple. Henceforth, the people of the old covenant looked backward more than forward. In Stephen's view of leadership, that was unfortunate. The New Covenant called for action to help God's kingdom grow and expand, rather than just maintain itself. It was to be a covenant of the tabernacle, ready to move on, rather than of the temple, expecting to stay put and waiting to be made more comfortable and ornate.

The leadership question for Trinity Church is whether this specific people will lean toward a tabernacle covenant or a temple covenant. The administrative action with the $50,000 will help determine the answer. They have a significant new resource. They can recognize some existing needs among the members. But what are the goals? Where are they going on the next leg of their common journey? What tasks do they want to set out for themselves?

If I were Pastor Westin, I would use this "problem" of the gift to focus the congregation's attention on a vision for the future. As an administrator, I would concentrate on helping them do this in active terms. Five or ten years down the road, what do they see themselves doing different from what they are doing now? When together they have worked out these goals, then they can make an intelligent decision about matching this resource with the many needs that can be discovered within and beyond the congregation.

As a pastor, I would want the vision of congregational outcomes in the future to be shaped by what God is telling this congregation today. The council that will consider the immediate situation should certainly pray. But they also ought to search God's word for guidance.

St. Paul's description of goals for church life in Ephesians 4:12–16 is a good place to look. He wanted "to equip the saints for the work of ministry, for building up the body of Christ." Paul wanted the body to reach to the very height of the fullness of Christ.

What works of ministry would the saints at Trinity church be doing if they were better equipped? What would their body of Christ look like if it were built-up more? Decisions should be made about the parts to emphasize. What would it mean for these Christians in that time and place to reach to the very height of the fullness of Christ? Choices should be made about where they will try to reach the highest.

The Journey and the Helmsman/Administrator

For pastors considering the importance of the administrator role, the fundamental question is whether they see their church as being on a journey with a destination. If so, getting the people there is the work of the pastors as administrators.

The apostle Paul had this concept of leadership. It is built right into his Greek word we commonly translate as administration. He used it in his description of gifts in 1 Corinthians 12. Right after the gifts of healing and helping, he lists *kubernesis*, which literally means "helmsmanship."

Helmsman calls forth the image of a ship. Moving the rudder was the sailor's immediate task, a function not unlike getting resources distributed. But in the ancient world, the helmsman had a greater responsibility. He was really the navigator. We would call him the captain of the ship. Someone else usually owned the ship and established its purpose. The helmsman made sure it got where it was supposed to go and looked after the crew along the way.

The Greek word shows up in modern English as *cybernetics*. This word calls forth a sophisticated management image. It describes the science of automated controls. The thermostat is a simple example. Such a device has three basic functions. One is to recognize a standard or condition that is desired. Setting the thermostat at seventy-two degrees is such a destination. The second function is to assess the current situation to determine whether a need exists. A thermostat does this with a heat sensitive device that measures temperatures. The third function is to activate some corrective resource when a need is registered. The thermostat switches on the furnace when the existing temperature falls below the intended temperature.

These three functions also exist in the helmsmanship of a ship. The navigation reading of the current position guides the setting of the sails and the turning of the rudder. But the second and third functions take on their importance only when the first function is accomplished, that is, when a destination is determined. Without a destination, navigation and steering cannot be taken seriously.

Likewise with church administration. A church can use the resources of its members' time, energy, and money in many different ways. It can be a ship with much wheel spinning and many people trimming sails. Making the effort to recognize and assess needs is a wise step to give guidance to that activity. But needs have to be sorted out so that the most important ones receive the necessary attention. This happens best when they are related to goals, when the church has some destination it is trying to reach. Then the discussion of perceived current needs is most constructive.

Alternatives

Pastors who have difficulty taking the administrative role seriously are often leaders who do not have a sense of covenant and journey. Some see mostly individuals each out on his or her own personal journey. Then there is not much of a covenant to shape and administer. Fairness and consistency in mutual commitments become incidental.

Some see the congregation as a whole but stay so busy trying to keep it from falling apart that they lose a sense of journey. Then administration becomes a chore of doing whatever has to be done to keep people happy. The ministry of such service is easy to overlook.

Some like to see movement but cannot focus on a clear vision of where the church should go. Then they get overwhelmed by all the possibilities they see and the conflicts that emerge. Administration becomes a series of frustrations that are preferably avoided.

When pastoral administration becomes a ministry to a people strengthening their covenant to move into a future God has for them, then it is worth taking seriously.

Summary

Mrs. Frye's generous gift would be celebrated by any pastor. All would want to affirm her for this act of devotion. But it should not be seen as just an individual act or only as an offering to God. Southard and Luecke readily recognize it also as a gift to fellow church members for their shared life in the Lord. This perception calls for an administrative response.

As a support-oriented administrator, Southard reacts to opportunities a church has as ways to give concrete meaning to its love as a body. The exercise of justice is basic to such Christian love. Administrators can promote the practice of love with justice through facilitating decision making that takes into account the needs and interests of others who could be affected by any action in the body. Supporting equitable relationships, pastoral administrators can contribute a process of doing theology in the life of the church.

As a task-oriented administrator, Luecke reacts to opportunities a congregation has as ways to move as far as it can to achieve its full potential as God's people seeking his will. Theirs is a covenant relationship that should remain open for movement into the future. The challenge is to expand ministries toward goals beyond current needs and interests. Identifying tasks to these ends, pastoral administrators can contribute guidance for building the body of Christ.

Administrators make linkages between resources, needs, and goals. Stewardship of resources is basic to all administration. Support leaders tend instinctively to link them with needs. Task leaders tend instinctively to focus on the linkages with goals.

3

Why Pastoral Administration Is So Important Today

The Nominations Committee

Pastor Claus was sitting in his study, in a reflective mood. He was preparing for the meeting of the nominations committee that evening. He had a document in each hand. One was the membership roster for New Hope Church. The other was the list of positions they were supposed to fill. It was attached to a copy of the church's constitution and bylaws that explained the duties of these positions.

"There has to be a better way to do this," Pastor Claus thought. "I am beginning to dread this annual roundup and review. Something must be wrong with what we are doing here." He was trying to make up his mind whether to share his reservations with the group.

When he first took the organizational list in hand that morning, he had a feeling of pride. Altogether, the church had sixty positions for a dozen boards and committees. Twenty-four were due for appointment. The church was certainly well organized, and he had helped develop the structure. But the more he thought about it, the more he recognized in himself a feeling of frustration.

Looking at the membership roster, he had to fight off a feeling of guilt. There was an individual story that went with each name. As pastor, he knew the stories pretty well. Most of the people did not need another intrusion in their busy lives. Yet, as good souls, most would agree to serve in the positions they were asked to fill.

What particularly bothered Pastor Claus was an absence of joy in most of the organizational process that had been set up. He recalled the dozens and dozens of meetings he attended last year. The dominant image he got was of tired men and women sitting around a table after a full day's work, trying to figure out why they were there and what they were supposed to do. He thought of the many seemingly endless, rambling discussions that never quite got anywhere.

This was the grim side of church work. He knew it, and they probably did, too. Meetings seldom had full attendance. It was clear that many of the meetings were not run well. Often there was no agenda. What continually surprised him was how even the successful businessmen often floundered in those meetings. They often seemed to be there for some reason other than the matters at hand.

Pastor Claus thought about comments from pastors of his grandfather's age. They talked of church life that seemed so much simpler, with a few trustees and one or two boards that met occasionally. He wondered whether church life today is really any richer or better.

"But what are the alternatives?" he asked himself. "We have to keep our members involved. If I show my concern tonight, we might end up with another committee to study the matter. Will I just make the problem worse?"

LUECKE

To Structure the Organizational Tool

Pastor Claus is to be commended for feeling uneasy about the organizational machinery at New Hope Church. He reflects solid pastoral instincts.

If a little bit of church organization is good, a lot is not necessarily better. It is somewhat like fertilizer. Too little causes the plants to struggle maintaining themselves. But too much will burn them out, leaving the lawn in worse shape than with no help at all. The right amount can help a lawn grow green and thick.

A better analogy is to say that an organization is a tool. It is a social structure that serves as a means to an end. Like any tool, it can be used clumsily, doing more damage than good. Learning how to use tools is basic to becoming a competent craftsman. Administration is the craft of assuring that an organization serves its intended purpose. The administrative role of leadership invites a pastor to become a better organizational craftsman.

As Pastor Claus frets about his church people and church organization, he has several options. One is to try to tighten up the organization. Or he can send signals that the organization is already too intrusive and should not be taken so seriously. Or he can explore other ways of organizing that will reduce the frustration and guilt yet still get the job done.

Tightening up church organization is easy—on paper. Position descriptions can be written more clearly and explicitly. Objectives can be clarified and polished. Meetings can be planned more carefully, with increased emphasis on detailed agendas and adherence to time constraints. If committees cannot figure out what they are supposed to do, good church administration can revolve around reducing such uncertainty.

But going that route will inevitably involve more organizational time and energy for many people, Pastor Claus most of all. The basic question pastors should ask is whether that much effort is really worthwhile. Most pastors do ask this question in their own minds, and, instinctively, they come to a negative answer. Other things seem more important in church life. Such a stance has merit, for reasons I want to highlight in this chapter.

The pastoral instinct often leans toward the other option—reducing the organizational intrusion. That, too, is easy to do—not so much on paper but more in practice. Boards, committees, positions, and decision-making processes can all be neglected or given minimal attention month after month. When everyone, including the pastor, is busy, it is quite reasonable to cancel meetings, to make up agendas after the group is together, or to leave projects unfinished. "You won't have to do much" is an attractive promise to members recruited to organizational positions.

But is such neglect good administration? Perhaps so. According to one axiom: If there isn't a good reason to meet, don't. Then the basic question becomes one of why the organizational apparatus should exist in the first place. Yet, for most churches in our current American culture, doing away with the formalities of boards, committees, and positions does not seem attractive. In many denominations, an organizational structure of some sort or another is prescribed. The invitation to frustration seems unavoidable.

What about the third alternative held out for our Pastor Claus? This is to explore other forms of organization that will reduce the frustration and guilt and still get the job done. To pursue this, pastors and church leaders need to answer for themselves the fundamental questions of the purposes the church's organizational dimension is supposed to serve. When "the job" to be accomplished is in focus, then a variety of designs to get it done can be more readily recognized.

Contributing to such creative design is why the craft of administration is so important in churches today.

Distinguishing Between Church and Organization

The function of church administration and church organization can be described as follows:

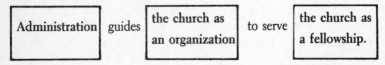

| Administration | guides | the church as an organization | to serve | the church as a fellowship. |

Administration, or management, cannot properly be spoken of apart from an organization (administrator and manager will be used interchangeably here). While we sometimes talk of someone managing his or her own time or ministry, this is not the usual meaning associated with the role of administrator. Acting in the manager role is consciously to develop and maintain specialized environments intended to coordinate the activities of people pursuing common purposes. As such, an organization is a deliberately designed, goal-oriented pattern of expectations and relationships that sets a context for what people do together. Administrators manage this specialized environment.

A common weakness among church leaders is a poor distinction between organization and church. Thus, what they are managing gets confused.

The confusion is somewhat like that between a physical building and a church. When many think about a church, they get an image of a building with a steeple and stained-glass windows. But, of course, in any New Testament theological sense, the church is the people who gather together and not the physical environment where they meet.

The organizational environment of a church is harder to distinguish from the church as a fellowship because it is made up of people, indeed, many of the same people who are also the church as a fellowship. The difference is that in the organization these people act and relate to others in designated positions according to predetermined expectations. In their organizational capacity, they perform specialized roles, be it elder, deacon, trustee, secretary, committee member, treasurer, administrator, or whatever role is formally recognized.

Just as there is more to a church than a physical building, there is more to a church than the organizational form it takes. Not every member of the church gathered as the congregation is part of the church organization, which is just the members who accept special responsibilities. Even then, for organizational participants, the performance of their organizational role may be just a fraction of their involvement in church life. Within the fellowship, there is usually much sharing of prayer, Bible study, exhortation, or service that never gets touched by the organization. When John, Sally, Jim, and Mary have dinner together and talk about what God is doing in their lives, they are doing church in the most fundamental sense, just as Carl and Ann may when they act out their Christian love by caring for an ailing neighbor. Such fellowship sharing may go on without a formal organization and, if one exists, may never be known in the formal processes.

Theologian Emil Brunner highlights this distinction in *The Misunderstanding of the Church.* [1] His thesis is that since the earliest centuries of the Christian church, theologians have looked at the church and seen an institution or organization. They then argue about what the institution should or should not do. The great Reformers, Luther and Calvin, saw the limits of the institution, but they settled for describing the extra dimension as the "hidden" or "invisible" church. Yet, that church is not hidden, it is made up of very visible people. It is just that they have been interacting in Spirit-led fellowship prior, in concept, to institutional forms. This is the basic *ekklesia.* Jurgen Moltmann develops this thesis in his contrast between "the church as an event" under the power of the Holy Spirit and "the church as an institution," which gives the event continuity and form.[2]

From a more behavioral perspective, this distinction can be expressed as the difference between primary and secondary relationships. The church as a "communion of saints" is the primary relationship of believers drawn together by the Holy Spirit and sharing a variety of worship, learning, witnessing, and serving responses to God's call in Christ. The church as an organization, if a fellowship has one, is a set of secondary relationships intended to help shape the primary ones.

Why bother with this distinction? Because the church as the primary fellowship gives purpose to the secondary church organization. A formal organization needs continually to justify its existence, which it does by accomplishing its intended goals. The goals of a church organization have something to do with serving a particular fellowship or community of Christians by helping to preserve it and build it up. To the extent that the community maintains itself and flourishes in its shared responses to God, the organization serving it is doing its job.

The two expressions of the church—the primary community and its secondary organization—are like two forms of a city. The city of Sunnydale may be fifty thousand people who live, work, and interact in a geographic area. It may also be a corporation with offices, committees, and budgets. Few of the residents are active in the corporation. Many do not even vote or pay taxes, but they are still in the community. All the activities of the community members far exceed the few points of common interest touched by the few active participants in the corporation. The measure of success of the secondary organization is the welfare of the primary community.

As presented earlier, the administrator's attention flows to the church organization, which then gives attention to the church as a fellowship. The reverse flow sets the purposes. Where the fellowship or community recognizes needs for special attention, it formalizes organizational relationships with the goal of meeting those needs. When the secondary relationships get complicated, the organization needs to be administered so that these organizational purposes get accomplished.

The Growing Need for Church Organization

A pastor once sketched out for me from his own experience the difference between these two expressions of a church.

He had served a pastorate in San Diego. He got quite used to a highly organized church life with many committees, meetings, and programs. A large percentage of members, including himself, put considerable energy into planning and running programs. "We had lots of organizational rah-rah," he said.

Then in the mid-1970s, he took a call to a large Lutheran congregation in semirural Illinois. He spent several years trying to get this church organized. It did not even have a budget, let alone the customary committees. But he encountered considerable passive resistance because the people did not see the need. Finally, he figured out they were right; their church life was indeed quite healthy by normal standards. With this realization, he relaxed and got on with other ministries among them.

The Illinois congregation was a well-established Christian community. There happened to be considerable overlap between the fellowship of believers and the small-town community where they lived and worked together. Even though the congregation numbered close to eight hundred, most felt they knew each other. They probably did, because the membership was so stable over the decades. When needs arose, a few elders would put out the word, and people responded. Effective leadership happened informally. A rational organizational structure of positions, objectives, responsibilities, and prescribed relationships had little to offer. This church did not need much administrative attention.

This pastor's San Diego congregation was the opposite in several important ways. While these Christians had a desire for fellowship, they consciously had to shape it over and over again. This was because of the constant change in membership, reflecting a highly mobile suburban community. An active and retired military population contributed to that mobility. They also brought a heightened sense of formal organization. Indeed, most members made their living in some sort of corporation or bureaucracy. Their instinctive response to problems in their fellowship life together was to define objectives and rationally to structure positions and relationships. Their fellowship was undoubtedly richer for all this planning and organizing. The pastor also had to be an effective administrator to help keep the organizational wheels moving.

This pastor's experience was unusual. He had taken a step back in time and touched two extremes in the process. Twentieth-century American church life is characterized by the opposite movement: from rural/small town to urban/suburban, from stability to mobility, from relatively close-knit neighborhoods and ethnic groups to few "natural" social groupings at all.

When Pastor Claus reflected on the simpler church life and ministry described by his grandfather, he was noting a time when congregations had less need for help structuring their routine interactions. Primary fellowship could happen with less attention from secondary organization. Church people brought with them a sense of relationships that supported the community.

The underlying reasons for the growing need for church organization are variations on the theme that our whole late twentieth-century American culture is losing its sense of community. We are becoming a people who find it hard to make long-term commitments to others, and we are losing the habits that used to allow sustained interaction to occur with seemingly little effort. Fundamental cultural shifts have left neighborhoods, schools, and community institutions of all sorts struggling to maintain themselves.

That church members can develop fellowship on their own, without organizational help, is an assumption that is perhaps most precarious today among church bodies that rely heavily on long-standing traditions to shape fellowship life. Traditions can provide a highly developed structure where traditional—i.e., nonadministrative—ministry could be quite effective. But whether as a cause or a consequence of the forces pulling people apart, adherence to the traditions that held them together has become much weaker in our culture today. The churches that pride themselves on historical polity and practices may discover that their structural strength is disappearing. They will have a special need to discover organizational ministries that can furnish fellowship structure in creative new ways.

Choosing an Organization

As Pastor Claus wrestled with his feelings about the formal organization of the New Hope community, he was really asking whether they had developed the right kind of organization to serve the fellowship. There are options. The differences cover not just alternative specific configurations and assignments. There are major differences in the way a formal organization is conceptualized. These theoretical assumptions determine to a great extent how organizational leaders go about their tasks. Skillful administration has risen in importance in church life today to avoid letting a community be victimized by the organizational theory it adopts. It takes a good craftsman to know which to use.

Five major models or theories of organization are commonly recognized today: [3] traditional, charismatic, classical, human relations, and systems. Each of these can be looked at theologically. Peter Rudge, writing from the context of the Church of England, has made a major contribution to such understanding. In *Ministry and Management*, he looks at each from the perspective of Christian doctrines of church, ministry, God, and man.[4] I cite his work not to explore it here but simply to note that there can be theology for each theory.

For Pastor Claus and most pastors today, I would advocate the *systems* theory as the model to guide their administrative thinking in the church. It is really a synthesis of the others, with some important insights that can open up fresh approaches to organizing church life. Exploring the other four will help set the context.

The traditional and charismatic models represent a prerational stage of thinking about organization. That is, goals, positions, relationships, and expectations are not consciously planned out and evaluated by the participants. The administrative role remains minimally developed.

Most small congregations probably still function within an organizational theory that relies on *traditions* to structure the patterns of interaction. The model is most evident in ethnic churches, like the Lutheran one described earlier. Expectations revolve around continuing what was done in the past. Decision making is simplified, since few alternative courses of action are recognized. Little formal communication is necessary, because the tradition is presumed to be known and shared by all. The year-by-year objectives really revolve around maintaining customary ways of doing things.

The *charismatic* theory received its name from sociologist Max Weber. The term focuses on leadership dynamics. Its use here is slightly different from its application to the charismatic movement, although this model is dominant in small Pentecostal churches. The emphasis is on the magnetism of a gifted leader, who shapes the expectations and relationships of the followers according to his intuition, presumably grounded in Scripture. The decision-making process revolves around shared, instantaneous, Spirit-led perception, often announced as a prophetic message. Formal, rational processes of setting goals, formulating rules, and determining authority positions are usually considered unnecessary. Indeed, formalities of this sort are often strongly resisted as institutional encroachment on the spontaneous feelings that are expected to integrate participants. Such fellowships have an organization of sorts, but the organization is hard to recognize according to the criteria associated with the concept in current usage.

When church leaders concentrate on a rationally developed organization, they have usually drawn on the classical or human relations models to guide their design.

The *classical* theory is also known as the bureaucratic model. It is the easiest to understand and the most prevalent across the wide range of society's organizations, even though the term bureaucracy has acquired heavy negative connotations. Bureaucracy simply means "power of the office." This way of thinking concentrates on defining ideal specialized positions, or offices, and then formally designating the authority and duties assigned to the people who find themselves holding each position. The design is usually made in the abstract, that is, without considering the strengths and interests of the unique individuals who will "staff" the organization. Policies and rules are relied upon to govern the interaction of the participants, providing a predictability that is highly valued. The authority of each position is limited and is presumed to be granted and coordinated by a higher level of authority, which is important to recognize and define. This arrangement is known as a hierarchy. The classical model draws much of its images from the world of machines. Administering it amounts to keeping the wheels moving.

When Pastor Claus was reflecting on the organization of New Hope Church, he was probably looking at the results of classical thinking. A tip-off is the rational outline provided in the constitution and bylaws, which present a legal base that is fundamental to this model. The advantage is that everyone can know what is *supposed* to happen.

The disadvantages become apparent when the ideal hits the reality of the differentially talented and motivated people who get fitted into this machinelike structure. Their understanding of and commitment to the tasks laid out will vary considerably, especially when they are not dependent on the organization to meet their personal needs. Thus, there is frequently a big gap between the stated organizational expectations and what is actually done by people who can appear quite half-hearted about the effort. Feelings of inertia, frustration, and guilt often abound. These are particularly troublesome feelings in churches.

The *human relations* model does not lend itself to precise description. Its secularly developed assumptions and techniques became quite popular among professionally trained ministers who addressed church organization in the 1960s and 1970s. Where the classical model stresses positions, this approach emphasizes groups and processes. It is a direct reaction to the limits of bureaucratic thinking.

In human relations thinking, organizational leadership amounts to forming groups and facilitating the dynamics of face-to-face interaction among people who share common interests. A high value is placed on informal and fluid relationships within and between groups. This is because of the assumption that the momentum of the organization comes from the various initiatives that arise from participants expressing their personal needs and opinions. The aim is to develop situations where they will share feelings and desires and then personally take the initiative to fulfill them. Goals are not given; they emerge. Decision making is a continuous process of coming to a common mind within the groups and then among the groups. Participative decision making is seen as the key to mobilizing energy and commitment to common effort. Administration amounts to facilitating the participatory process.

The classical model can be caricatured as an organization without people. The human relations model almost becomes people without organization. More precisely, the organization becomes a loose network of groups, a framework within which they carry out their processes.

A tip-off to the presence of human relations thinking in a church is the presence of dozens and dozens of committees. Whenever there is a problem or a need, the instinctive administrative response is to form a group to take care of it, and the number has a way of mushrooming. Pastor Claus may have some of these instincts.

Churches using human relations thinking eventually discover several outcomes. One is growing confusion as groups overlap and participants lose track of who is doing what. More serious, though, is a sense of frustration with implementation. The participatory process stresses preparatory discussion and is not oriented toward consistent action. It yields a multiplicity of subjective goals which do not necessarily translate into movement toward achieving a few goals shared by all. As one church leader expressed his experience, the process eventually runs into a wall; the presumed commitment to action too often does not appear.

With the hindsight of experience, one can question whether the human relations techniques for the participatory group decision-making process is often more of a hindrance than a help to the primary fellowship. The burden of seemingly endless hours of process can drag an organization to the ground before it ever produces a lasting payoff for the effort. The test for the energy used in developing organization is whether the fellowship flourishes in its shared life of worship, learning, witnessing, and serving. There are more direct ways to support and guide the interaction of Christians in fellowship.

Systems Thinking about Church Life

Three scriptural insights provide the basis for a way of thinking about church organization that is neither classical nor human relations. They came from the apostle Paul, and all are presented in the twelfth chapter of 1 Corinthians.

One is the fundamental concept of the church as the body of Christ. The second is the understanding of the Holy Spirit as the source of energy in church life. The third is recognition of members as manifesting a diversity of gifts given by the Spirit for the common good.

1. The body of Christ is a wonderful image for what today is called systems theory. This model is now dominant in the study of organizations as done in schools of management. To describe something as a system is to recognize the presence of many different parts or participants that act in interdependent relationships and that fit together as a whole greater than the sum of the parts.

There are few descriptions of a system better than the one Paul offered long ago, and, of course, he was explaining a church:

> The body does not consist of one member but many. . . . God arranged the organs in the body, each one of them, as he chose. . . . The eye cannot say to the hand, "I have no need of you," nor again the head to the feet, "I have no need of you.". . . If one member suffers, all suffer together; if one member is honored, all rejoice together" (1 Cor. 12:14–26).

The systems model of today emerged from the biological study of living organisms that function naturally on their own, unlike the classical model with its images of machines built according to prescribed relationships derived from abstract principles. Organic theory is another name for the systems model, in contrast to mechanistic theory.

Systems thinking concentrates on understanding both the purposes that give pattern to the interdependencies and the environment to which the system must adapt. This approach looks at relationships with the assumption that a functioning system already exists, meaning that there is some sort of effective balance of relationships within the system and between the system and its environment. The task of organizational leadership is to intervene when external changes threaten the balance or when internal components are no longer contributing effectively to the larger system. Leaders guide adaptation to change. They do this by continually clarifying basic purposes and interpreting changes for the participants so they can respond sensibly and continue to fulfill their purpose that brought them into the system.

In systems language, people in organizational positions form the management subsystem that monitors change and tries to shape system responses. Where there is little change, there is little need for the managerial subsystem and its administrators.

For churches, systems thinking is an advance over the classical model because it starts with people already in fellowship—the body of Christ gathered as a congregation. The organizational management subsystem, if there is one, adapts itself to the existing fellowship rather than trying to adapt the fellowship to its organization. It is an advancement over the human relations model because it stresses the interdependence of all the possible groups yet does not pretend that decisions can be made only when all parts agree; some are the head while others are the feet.

2. What the systems theory does not address is how a system comes into existence. This is an important advantage theologically. The classical model tries to explain beginnings by sketching out an ideal set of relationships and encouraging people to perform accordingly. The human relations model tries to make a system emerge by using the participatory process to elicit commitment to common effort.

But, especially in churches, such beginnings are just not an organizational problem. God creates the system, through the Holy Spirit, just as God creates the living system of a plant or a human body. As Paul says, "There are varieties of working, but it is the same God who inspires [gives energy to] them all" (1 Cor. 12:6). Neither the classical nor the human relations model provides much room for seeing God's direct involvement in an organization. The systems model does. The organization simply recognizes the relationships generated by the Spirit and then tries to guide them.

The first Christian church appeared at Pentecost, when people were filled with the Holy Spirit. Then, according to the description in Acts 2:44, "All who believed were together and had all things in common." It seemed to happen spontaneously. We have to assume that among the individuals there was a readiness to share, to come together. It is hard to see how that first response could be contrived by authority relationships or made to evolve through deliberative processes. When they believed, these first Christians felt like a body and started acting like one. The reader is clearly meant to conclude that the Holy Spirit made it happen. The Acts account goes on to tell the story of how the first system developed its managerial subsystem, including food administrators who coped with changes in distribution patterns.

This relatively spontaneous sharing, or fellowship, is how churches as systems still happen today.

3. Within a systems perspective, organizational leadership is the task of clarifying purposes and highlighting needs so that system participants can respond. Understanding the working parts of the system is key to guiding the energy of the workers into more effective responses to the needs of the system.

The apostle Paul presents a uniquely Christian understanding of the working parts of a church system. These are the believers who each in his or her own way are gifted by the Spirit to contribute something to the body. As Paul said:

Now there are varieties of gifts, but the same Spirit; and there are varieties of service, but the same Lord; . . . To each is given the manifestation of the Spirit for the common good. . . . All these [believers] are inspired by one and the same Spirit, who apportions to each one individually as he wills (1 Cor. 12:4–7, 11).

In this Corinthian epistle, as well as in Ephesians and Romans, Paul offers a helpful description of the variety of God-gifted workers. They include apostles, prophets, teachers, healers, administrators, helpers, hosts, shepherds, and many others. Paul's message to the congregations he led was that the individual members should recognize their special gifts and get on with using them.

Peter, his apostolic colleague, understood the same system dynamics. He also clarified the administrative task that goes with this theological expression of organization theory. In 1 Peter 4:10, he exhorted, "As each has received a gift, employ it for one another, as good stewards of God's varied grace." Individuals have a personal stewardship responsibility. But the whole body also needs to practice good stewardship of the working parts given it. Such stewardship is another name for administration.

There is considerably more to be said about the administrative implications of seeing spiritual gifts as the organizing principle in the body of Christ. I will pursue this in the next chapter.

Back to Pastor Claus

All of these theories about church and organization got beyond Pastor Claus and his upcoming meeting of the nominating committee. We left him sitting in his office, considering what to do about his pastoral frustrations with New Hope's organization.

The main message is that he should respect his pastoral instincts. In his administrative role, he should express those instincts in ways that will help the formal organization adapt to the realities of their current church life. What seemed to work a few years ago may not be working now. By probing purposes, he can reduce the possibility that the fellowship members are becoming captives of their organization.

If committee members find their assignment an intrusion on their time, they were probably asked to function in a way that does not match their gifts. Maybe they do not need to be in an organized group at all to make their contribution. Others in the organization, like the members of the nominating committee, could help them discover what they are ready to do. Perhaps the nominating committee should become a personnel development committee, overseeing the stewardship of spiritual gifts.

If a committee is not functioning well, it may not perceive a real need that merits their attention. Indeed, there may not be a significant need if that part of church life is going well. Then the committee could be excused for the time being.

If meetings get sidetracked because members want to spend their time visiting with each other, maybe the church needs fewer meetings for these secondary relationships and more occasions for the participants to gather in primary relationships of sharing and support.

Maybe the congregation does not need all of the boards and committees in the first place. God may have gifted this church with enough talented administrators who can take personal responsibility to provide the necessary fellowship-building leadership in the various areas of concern.

Churches have organizational options. Pastors who understand administration can help keep the organization a servant of the fellowship.

If I were Pastor Claus, I would go ahead and raise questions when the nominating committee meets. I would probe purposes and explore alternatives. This is how systems are stimulated to adapt and keep themselves healthy.

SOUTHARD

To Hold the Organization Accountable

Pastor Claus and his leaders are floundering in a church life that is in danger of misidentifying its source of corporate energy. They have allowed themselves to think that their organization is a solution in itself. They failed to distinguish between the church as the body of Christ and the organization that supports the body.

Without this distinction, it is easy to misidentify church structures with spiritual reality. A prescribed pattern of relationships and a particular style of leadership can then appear to be the embodiment of God's will for that congregation. The organization is absolutized and alternative notions of reality and power are overlooked. Such blind management too often struggles to stabilize and expand the structure in such a way that it is not considered to be just an organization but becomes the only possible reality of God at work in the church. The ultimate result of this illusion is to place the church's welfare almost completely in the hands of the pastor and appointed church leaders as custodians of an inflexible organization.

How to prevent this is a concern Luecke and I share. The most evident solution is to seek the leadership of a pastor who understands how church organization can be kept in service to the life of the Spirit. This is basic to the role of pastoral administrator. We both see the importance of flexible response to the needs of the whole body.

In his structuralist approach, Luecke stresses the importance of mastering the organization by knowing the structural alternatives and avoiding their excesses. He is prone to assume the pastoral identity of the minister and urge better administration through better organizing.

I am inclined to assume that the organizing function of administration is more effective when the pastoral function is better understood. The way to be a better pastoral administrator is to be a better pastor. This role is so important in the church today because pastoral insights and sensitivities are so easily lost in proliferating organizational distractions.

We live in a complex, technological society in which organizations are necessary for stable and understandable relationships between people. But the organizations may become so complex and overpowering that they lose their original purpose and contribute to alienation and obscurity. Since church members live in such a society, the church must develop appropriate organizations to intersect with other organizations and to build up the body of Christ through patterns of relationships with which people are familiar.

Competent pastoral administration is necessary so that through organization love, power, and justice can appear in the church in their natural order. The love of God and neighbor has to be the basic purpose for which all procedures are developed to maintain the life of the body of Christ. The power of love is to be expressed in the just distribution of services to individuals according to their needs and the purposes of the church. Because the power is in God's love rather than in organizational form, flexibility and freedom should be maximized. When we distinguish God's power from the support arrangements of organization, we are free to choose any organizational structure that will serve the body of Christ at a particular time and in a particular culture.

We must continually ask why it is necessary to organize at all. There is no need in the body of Christ for any structure that does not express the many-faceted wisdom of God (Eph. 3:7–13).

Yet, out of Paul's command to express God's wisdom in many forms, we can actually recognize that some organization is necessary. Without the constraints of organizational procedures, special interests may arise and individual desires may dominate some aspects of the church's life with a consequent neglect of many others. Unrestrained individualism or the development of cliques can be minimized by a multifaceted organization that meets a variety of needs through common commitment to God's love in Christ. Basically, the need for organization is to be found in the church's recognition that sin is a constant threat both within the body of Christ and in the world.

In the Book of Acts, organization occurs first to apply love with justice, but then it also appears to concentrate the church's power in certain ways, such as in the support of missionaries. The human resource of individuals are limited even when they are channels of God's grace. The use of God's gifts, and the prevention of their misuse, is another purpose of church organization.

Pastoral sensitivity to people as they are accentuates these two purposes of church organization: to facilitate a variety of forms of love in action, despite sin, and to channel ways for individuals to use the gifts God gives them. Holding the organization accountable to these purposes is a good reason to give serious pastoral effort to administering the organization.

Accountability is a key word in any pastoral approach to Christian maturity. But the opportunity for personal growth and satisfaction in accomplishment is often lost in the human relations approach to administration. This is popular with pastors who have my type of training and disposition; that is, we become so "sensitive" to the needs of individuals that we give all our emphasis to acceptance and none to accountability. This is really a very immature form of counseling, since it allows our client to stagnate "inside" with no realistic guidance or the achievement of goals that would benefit both the person and society. The problem is perpetuated among those who have sought the church as a place of refuge and who continually ask, "Why didn't I get my fair share out of life?" This is an important question to be explored in counseling, along with another question, What do I owe to life?

When we are willing to balance both of these questions, we will not only be more mature counselors, but we will also see how responsibility in organization is related to personal maturity. Ideally, we cannot have one without having the other.

When we combine both of these questions in church management, we can be specific about the accountability of individual church members. This brings a sense of accommodation of their individual needs and talents with specific opportunities of service through the church and the kingdom of God. Our question to all members of the body of Christ can be, What is the form of love that you can most appropriately embrace in our fellowship? Through this question, we offer an opportunity for commitment that is stable and satisfying because some thought is given to the varying interests and talents of members and to the varieties of objectives that can be met through a fully formed church.

Organizing the Forms of Love in Action

What are the formulations of God's love in the church that will express his divine purposes in relation to the specific gifts and grace of each member of his body? The meeting place of specific organizational structures and the general goals of a body of believers can be expressed in both theological and sociological terms.

Theologically, love in action through the church is called "the manifold wisdom of God" (Eph. 3:10).[5] This manifestation of God's divine plan grows in our hearts (Eph. 3:18) and is implemented in our calling, our combination of gracious relationships (4:1–2) with the use of specific gifts (4:11 f.) through the body of Christ. Ephesians 3:10 is translated in the Good News Version as "God's wisdom in all its different forms."

The organizational form of "manifold" wisdom is not specified in the New Testament (although denominations have claimed to uphold "the New Testament pattern" of organization).[6] Instead, we can search the Scriptures for God's general purposes that are to be served through the church. In sociological language, these general purposes of an organization are called "pattern variables." This is the name given by sociologist Talcott Parsons to the overall requirements of any system that holds people together as they perform a mission in society. Patterns are general themes that are woven into a variety of recognizable programs. They are never to be identified with any one form of an organization in one time and place. They are the reasons behind the various functions of an institution.[7]

I think of these pattern variables as a modern application of

Paul's statement about the work of God's power through the church "in all its different forms." Each "form" is a part of God's wisdom, so long as each is subordinate to his eternal purpose achieved through Christ Jesus our Lord (Eph. 3:7–13). In organizational terms, these pattern variables are pattern maintenance, integration, adaptation, and goal attainment.

How can we combine the theological and sociological explanations by which a body of believers can express divine and human purposes? At least four forms may be found from phrases in the New Testament that relate to the church and our fellowship in it.

1. As "God's own people," the church is to maintain God's own character in holiness and love. Our mission is to keep intact and accurate the message of the gospel through the qualities of corporate life (1 Pet. 2:9; 1 John 4:8). The basic question for the church is: What did Christ do, and what, if anything, is he still doing? The church is the agency of society that proclaims the life, death, and resurrection of Jesus as Christ. This agency is to be maintained against the lures of lesser or different objectives.

2. As the "fellowship in the Spirit," the church is organized for support and instruction of those who aspire to faithfulness. These combined purposes are presented in the assembly after Pentecost: "And they devoted themselves to the apostles' teaching and fellowship, to the breaking of bread and the prayers" (Acts 2:42).

Fellowship is more than a friendly association. It is participation in something with someone else. The new element in Christian fellowship is the Holy Spirit. L. S. Thornton translates Paul's benediction in 2 Corinthians 13:14 as "fellowship and participation in the Holy Spirit." For the Spirit is to be regarded not as the subject who brings us together in fellowship but rather as the object in which we all share, the focus of our common interest.[8]

One sign that the church is more than a sentimental association of homogeneous people is the willingness of each member to bear the burdens of another (Gal. 5:22–6:5). By mutual support, we proclaim the meaning of God's love. Through a sacrificial life, we know that we participate in the body of Christ, the Lord of life whom we proclaim (Phil. 2:1–13).

3. A sacrificial love is to be realistically applied to the needs of all people. Jurgen Moltmann has presented the practice of love by Christ as the sign of his messiahship both to the disciples of John and to all churches who claim an apostolic ministry. If a

person wishes to know which church organization is truly representative of Jesus, we will see the proclamation of his kingdom in the ministry of healing and the proclamation of the Good News to the poor (Matt. 10:8).[9] Those who serve as he did will suffer for it (John 15:18–27).

In organizational terms, this means that the church is to meet human need both through challenge and change, comfort and security.[10]

4. The church is an organization that can translate good intentions and religious commitment into specific, enduring programs that nurture the development of individuals and transform society. There is to be a "demonstration of the Spirit and power" (1 Cor. 2:4). A spiritual church has impact.

Organizationally, these forms mean a working church. Needs must be assessed, resources considered, projects planned, volunteers recruited, money secured, and schedules followed. A church with comprehensive spiritual power will continually relate program development and organization to these four forms of God's wisdom for his body: "God's own people," a "fellowship in the Spirit," a gathering of "suffering servants," and a "demonstration of the Spirit and power."

How will a church know if these purposes are being fulfilled? Look at the use of time and money. This is one of the ways through which an organization can graphically demonstrate the commitment of a congregation to one or more of God's purposes.

A few years after five new Presbyterian churches had been started in California, Donald Metz compared their initial high idealism with the flow of money and time. He found that in four of the churches there had been a subtle shift in priorities toward concrete, limited tasks that maintained a building and a staff for programs in that building. The process was so insidious that he called it "goal subversion."

One congregation avoided this spiritual stagnation by adopting specific emphases through small discussion groups. There was a continual reminder of primary Christian objectives such as sacrificial service, fellowship, and sharing. Each member was challenged to participate actively in these basic objectives of the church. As the church combined all of these emphases in positive programs, they spent more and more money in the wider community and developed a strong mission beyond their own congregation. As a result, there was a steady increase in benevolent giving because program support was related to the essential task of witnessing and sacrificial service. The leadership postponed any financial investment in a building for worship or Christian education. An overinvestment of time and money in a building program would have subverted other purposes of this Christian congregation.[11]

Organizing Around Grace and Gifts

How is a "multiform" church to be developed and maintained? We have just discussed one answer, which is the priority of theological goals above any support system for those goals, whether it be a building, a budget, a denominational program, or the priorities of any one group in the church.

A second answer is related to the first. Theological goals depend on the personal gifts and grace of members in the body of Christ. They come out of the primary relationships of the people in a congregation and give meaning and significance to the secondary relationships through committees, boards, and offices.

What do we mean by grace and gifts? Grace is given specific meaning in Galatians 5 as the fruit of the Spirit. Here Paul describes the qualities of attitude toward self and others that build up the body of Christ. The significance of grace for administration is twofold. First, any work done within the church must manifest the graciousness that was in the character of Christ. Second, in both leadership and membership of a church that grows in all ways toward Christ, the essential measure of church growth is Christian graciousness. In organizational terms, grace is quality control. The fruit of the Spirit defines the qualities of life that are to be identified with each person who is labeled as a Christian.

Gifts, however, are selective. They are all bestowed by God for the common good, but they are not found in equal amounts in every Christian. Even the listing of the gifts is diverse (Rom. 12:5; 1 Cor. 12; Eph. 4:12, 15–16).

If gifts are diverse, how can they be identified? A gift is identified by the gracious way in which a person contributes to the body of Christ. We can identify gifts both by presence and by absence. When spiritual gifts are contributed by each member, there is harmonious growth in the membership as all are edified (1 Cor. 14). When gifts are absent, especially the greatest gift of love, the lifelessness of the congregation is apparent (1 Cor. 13:1–3).

When grace and gifts are combined in building up the church, a multiform organization is inevitable. The four forms of God's purposes for the church are essential to the Christian growth of individuals. They are answers to the two basic questions of character: What has life contributed to me? What can I contribute to life? Or, to use the analogy of some of the parables of our Lord, a multiform church will provide seasons of sowing and seasons of reaping. So long as a church concentrates and depends upon the primary, personal growth of disciples, there will be direction and motivation toward all forms of church growth.

At the same time, this centering upon grace and gifts will prevent the spiritual aberrations of program pushing, budget dominance, and preoccupation with numbers that have often been associated with church growth and "successful" administration. Why? Because an overextension of any one purpose of the church will replace grace with manipulation and reduce the gifts to a set of secular talents that guarantee quantitative gain. Whenever a church loses Christian grace and spiritual gifts, there is a temptation to substitute slick promotional campaigns, make people feel guilty, and fill the worship service with announcements about budget deficits and committee meetings. These are signs that a church has lost both grace and gifts.

These organizational signs of spiritual stagnation can prompt a congregation to ask which programs or types of organizations depend upon gifts and grace versus programs and organizations that must be promoted, financed, and managed through techniques that are essentially manipulative. If any church program requires more than grace and gifts, then it has been overextended at the expense of other essential elements in the body of Christ.

Keeping Gifts and Grace Primary

How do we keep gifts and grace primary in the life of a congregation?

One answer is through leadership focus on questions such as that of Bishop D. T. Niles of Sri Lanka to the third assembly of the World Council of Churches: "Is the present form of church life a major hindrance to the work of evangelism?" His question led to the formation of study groups in North America and Europe who reported their findings in *Planning for Mission* and *The*

Missionary Structure of the Congregation. These were lively investigations of the way in which the body of Christ could challenge and contribute to the extension of love and the formation of justice in many areas of society. Several denominations established "experimental ministries" as a result of these studies and found that they were soon attracting into the church a variety of people who had felt outside of traditional church organizations and patterns of behavior.

A second answer is administratively to insist that a church cannot grow unless each person contributes his or her gift. This was the admonition of the apostle Paul to the Corinthian church. All bring a gift because all minister to each other. As Martin Luther rediscovered in his study of the New Testament, the royal priesthood spoken of in 1 Peter 2:9 is the priesthood of every believer to every other person. There is no exclusive priesthood that dispenses the means of grace to the congregation, for the means of grace are within each member for distribution to all.

A dependence upon grace and gifts in all the congregation will prevent distortions in church organization and program manipulation. The only possible programs in a church that depends upon spiritual gifts will be the programs that are prompted through those gifts. If members are not challenged, motivated, and trained to use their gifts for the general good through any one aspect of church life, then that function must remain dormant until God grants both gift and grace for implementation.

A relentless dependence on gifts within the body can revolutionize a church. Congregations can change from a hierarchical structure, in which a pastor is expected to do most of the work, into the common life of the body of Christ which creates a dynamic fellowship. I use the word *relentless* for this emphasis because conflict, abandonment, and death are part of this process. Old habits must die, both in the pastor and the people. Ancient dependency patterns must disintegrate. Prestigious programs and pet committees will perish. But those who are willing to let an organizational emphasis die for the sake of God's kingdom will find that the gifts bestowed by God will enrich all the congregation beyond any expectation.

Much has been written and demonstrated about the renewal of congregations through a dependence upon the gifted leadership of the laity. But not enough has been written about a distortion of the gifts, which is an overdependence upon special, showy gifts that are called "spiritual." This is a problem in some of the newer churches, which has often occurred in the history of the church. It is a preoccupation with spectacular healing, impulsive prophecies, and unrealistic expectations of zealous and immature leaders. Paul spoke of such people as "spiritually uninformed" (1 Cor. 12:1–2) and proceeded to describe a variety of gifts that were necessary for the full functioning of the body of Christ. He continually urged the use of all of these gifts and warned against prioritizing them. The failure of many churches to build up the body of Christ is because of their narrow-minded interpretation of gifts. Enthusiastic utterance and unworkable faith are given priority. Careful administration, faithful pastoral care, patient teaching, scholarly Bible teaching, and thoughtful prayer are discarded.

A third answer to the maintenance of grace and gifts as primary is to keep a balance between all of the church's purposes. An example of this need can be seen in the occasional disagreement of a pastor and lay leaders over the principal goals of a local congregation. The issue emerged in one form around the church's involvement in civil rights. Jeffrey Hadden found through questionnaires that two-thirds of the clergy but only one-third of the lay leadership would support clergy involvement in civil rights movements.[12] Other studies showed that clergy and laity agreed on such general purposes as worship and Christian education but diverged on other church functions, such as evangelism and social action.[13]

In many ways, these conflicts highlighted an emphasis upon the practical application of the gospel versus the proclamation of the gospel. Could these two basic purposes of the church be reconciled? The answer is in the realm of "grace." Thomas C. Campbell and Yoshio Fukuyama found that the most devout members of a congregation were most likely to favor action in the area of civil justice.[14] A meditation upon the qualities of Christ in the life of the believer led inevitably to a concern for those to whom the believer came to minister.

If a pastor does not depend upon Christian grace and gifts for the solution to differences in priorities, he or she may experience a widened gap between clergy expectation and parishioner performance. In seeking to solve the differences, a minister may be seduced away from an emphasis upon the primary relationships in the congregation, which are built upon grace, and overemphasize ecclesiastical office and power. Of course, it is difficult to exercise such fruits of the Spirit as long-suffering, patience, and kindness when a pastor finds members of the congregation insensitive to the poor and needy of the community. But these graces are essential to any enduring program of individual and social renewal.

William Nelson and William Lincoln, youthful associates in a traditional reformed church, testified from their own experience that commitment to a social action program was difficult to maintain without keeping a balance between other purposes of the church. A preoccupation with one aspect of Christian witnessing and a neglect of others was damaging both to this specific program and to the larger life of the congregation. People in the program began to be less and less committed as their natural enthusiasm waned and no spiritual source of renewal was tapped. Other members of the congregation began to complain that they were being treated as second-class Christians by those who were in social action. Finally, the young associate pastors admitted that the program could only be maintained by the continuing support of the senior pastor, who had always been a prophetic voice for social change. But he had also been a pastor to individuals and had honored the contribution of conservative members in the church's routine activities.[15]

There must not only be a balance between sacrificial service and the loving character of God's people. There must also be a combination of fellowship in the Spirit and a demonstration of power. People come into churches to fulfill a sense of community; and the church must always ask this question, To what *kind* of community is a Christian ministry directed? [16] When there is exclusive emphasis upon homogeneity, the result may be community comfort without Christian challenge.

To balance fellowship with prophecy, comfort with challenge, there must be as much dependence upon gifts in the congregation as there is upon grace. Those who are moved by God's Spirit to speak about injustice in the community and the increase of love in the congregation must be encouraged along with those who faithfully maintain programs and carefully balance contrary opinions. The apostle Paul spoke of the essential need for prophets to explain the unintelligible speech of some in the Corinthian church, so that the entire body might be edified and built-up. This provided education and fellowship. But in the same letter, Paul challenged wealthy members of the congregation to think about others as they participated in the Lord's Supper, and he warned them that thoughtless and selfish members of the congregation were in danger of sickness and death (1 Cor. 11).

This balance can only be maintained when graciousness discerns the needs of the whole body and gifts stir up and conform the body to the character of Christ. Grace Goodwin found in her study of church renewal that the congregations that changed in the direction of Christian mission and discipleship were those in which some individual, either a long-term lay leader or a respected pastor, had continually challenged the congregation to be more loving and sacrificial. These were people who had exercised their gifts for the good of the body and had shown through their gracious character the direction in which they expected the "good" to be expressed.[17]

A concern for the full functioning of the church will increase our dependence upon grace and gifts. At the same time, an equal emphasis upon grace and gifts will maintain a balance.[18] With such emphases, administration becomes an intentional movement of the body of Christ, based upon the motivation of love within each member for the just distribution of services for the common good.

Without this intentional administration, motivated by the Spirit of Christ, one church function may predominate over the others, some essential functions may be ignored, spectacular gifts may be emphasized to the exclusion of gifts for the common good, or the prophetic gift of love may be ignored while the congregation luxuriates in easy grace.

Summary

The administrator role becomes more important for a pastor as the organizational dimension becomes more evident in church life today. We both see that the leadership challenge is to keep the secondary relationships of organization in service to the primary functions and relationships of a church. The pastor cannot escape the responsibility to exercise such administrative leadership.

We have different explanations for why the organization is important. Luecke concentrates first on the presence and necessity of some sort of structure to shape relationships. When church people find it difficult informally to get together and to do what they feel called to do (as is increasingly happening in a society that is losing its sense of community), then they fall back on formal efforts to plan out rationally their intended relationships. This is organization, which is supposed to support the fellowship. Organization is a tool for the formation of a covenant. Southard concentrates first on support and sees two needs for organization. One is to provide familiar patterns of relationships to people who find themselves living in a complex, highly organized society. The other is to protect the diversity of membership interests and needs from dominance by special interests. Organization is a tool for the exercise of justice.

We have different emphases for how the pastoral administrator can keep the organizational tool aimed at its proper function. Luecke stresses skill in understanding and designing the organization and lays out conceptual alternatives for administrative craftsmen. Southard stresses pastoral sensitivity and insights and lays out theological purposes to which the administrator should hold the organization accountable. The structural emphasis tends to assume pastoral instincts of the administrator. The support approach tends to assume the organizational follow-through by the administrator.

In thinking about church organization, both see the primacy of diverse individuals as gifts given by the Spirit for the common good of the fellowship. Southard sees them as channels of God's grace, to be administratively supported and respected as the force for cohesiveness and renewal of church life. Luecke sees them as the working parts of the system of church life, to be administratively guided into the service of one another through the practice of good stewardship of God's varied gifts.

We can each agree with the other's views. We see them as complementary, arriving at similar outcomes from different directions.

4

A Personal View to Keep Administration Exciting

The Burned-Out Pastor

When I heard the voice of Jim, an old friend, calling long distance, I wondered if anything was wrong. No, he just wanted to call and see if I was getting established in my new church. He sounded confident and satisfied with his work. Yet, worry came through as we talked about several families that resented the dismissal of the minister of music, to whom they were all related. I knew from previous conversations that the minister of music was always "doing his own thing" and resisted any cooperation with my friend as the pastor. Finally, the choir and most of the ruling elders had agreed that the minister of music should be "retired."

Now the relatives had gathered around and spread stories in the congregation about the pastor's arbitrary temper and the unjust way in which the minister of music had been dismissed. A power struggle was beginning to surface.

"Well," concluded my friend, "I just wonder how much longer I should stay here. Maybe I should take off a year and begin training as a pastoral counselor."

I asked my friend to meet with me when we attended a pastors' conference in a few weeks.

The few weeks made a difference. My friend now spoke slowly and deliberately as we had dinner:

> I just don't know. I'm forty-five and have nowhere to go. Madge [his wife] says that I'm married to the church. Now that the kids are getting away from home, she wants to know when we'll have time together. I just don't know. She made me have a checkup because I wasn't sleeping well. The doc says I need a long vacation. But how can I take a month away from the church? It'll blow up! I've got to keep a steady helm, be at all the committee meetings, and see that things get done.
>
> The doc asked what "kicks" I get out of life. I didn't know. I used to enjoy fishing; but, when I sit still, I think about things to be done at the church. I worry too much, my wife says. She's wonderful, but I wonder how much of me she can take. I don't really enjoy anything anymore—well, maybe preaching when we have a good anthem and when somebody joins the church. But I just don't feel in charge of anything anymore; I'm just putting out fires. And I don't start anything, I'm not a program-thinker-upper like I used to be. We're just spinning our wheels, and they get clogged, and I have to oil the machinery all the time.
>
> To whom should I write about clinical training? Maybe I should be a full-time counselor. I think I could help people better that way.

SOUTHARD

To Reconcile the Weak and the Strong

Jim implies that his real motivation is in counseling individuals. Yet, his chief concerns in our conversations were task-oriented. He was discouraged because of organizational conflicts, and he was worried that he was losing interest in program development. Perhaps as a senior pastor, he is doing the wrong kind of ministry for his personal interests. But it could also be that he has not learned how to see administration as an extension of the interests that now professedly excite him.

Would Jim be more encouraged if he was shown how the insights of a counselor could be applied to the administrative concerns of his present pastorate?

How could he come to see this? I would start with a central administrative issue of the New Testament church—the conflict of the weak and the strong. This is a persistent problem in any church, and the solution requires some counseling skills in the recognition of individual differences among members, an ability to help each person accept his or her own strengths and weaknesses, and a presentation of the incentives for people of differing sentiments and abilities to work together. When Jim is challenged from this perspective, his manifest motivation for counseling can enrich his previous preoccupations with administrative tasks.

Working with Individual Differences

Let's begin the remotivation with a look at the necessity of working with individual differences in at least three ways: (1) to identify the weak and the strong; (2) to honor the weak and the strong who are gracious in the use of their gifts for the church; and (3) to develop policies and procedures by which the weak and the strong may work together.

These were pastoral skills called forth by the unique composition of the early church. Rich people came into homes where the poor and the slaves were gathered (James 2:1–13). The foolish and the weak gained leadership in a church that knew the meaning of wordly wisdom and status (1 Cor. 1:9, 26–31). The leadership of the church contained timid people who needed boldness (2 Tim. 1:7) and dominant people who needed to see humility (1 Pet. 5:3).

The church neither disregarded nor despised these differences. Instead, the fellowship developed an administrative design with major pastoral implications, by which the strong and weak, foolish and wise, timid and dominant should work together in the power of love and justice. This was the major theme of the last chapters of Romans.[1]

How does a pastor combine various shepherding skills and orientation to meet the same challenge in a twentieth-century church? Essentially, the same pastoral perspectives aid the administrative task.

Identify the Weak and the Strong

A national survey of Episcopalians concluded: "Parishioners whose life situations most deprive them of satisfaction and fulfillment in the secular society turn to the church for comfort and substitute rewards." [2]

In the Episcopalian survey, widows, retired people, and socially disadvantaged people found great comfort in Christian fellowship. Along with these, I would add those who are constitutionally dependent, the individuals who for psychological reasons have always been "weak." Both the situational and the constitutional sources of weakness will lead to a vested interest in maintaining the religious institution through which comfort and support is derived.[3]

When we honestly identify these differences, we can understand why people tend to despise those who are different. It is very easy for the "comforted" ones to envy the psychologically or socially advantaged people who are members of the congregation but are not very dependent upon its activities. The Episcopal study found the ideal of society, the upper-class young father, to be hardly involved in the church at all.[4] Perhaps this will help us to understand why the "weak" in the Roman church were condemning the "strong" for disregarding customs and the Christian-Jewish calendar (Rom. 14:5–10).

Those who see themselves as psychologically or societally weak or dependent upon the church organization will usually resist any change because of its possible threat to their security. A United Church of Christ study found less favorable attitudes toward other races among the socially disadvantaged people in the church.[5] As Grace Goodman found in her study of social change in Presbyterian churches, the church was like an ark of safety for many people in transient neighborhoods. Hence, the title of her study was *Rocking the Ark.*

Honor the Weak and the Strong

The socially disadvantaged can be helped to be less closed minded against the needs of others. The United Church of Christ study found that the most devout people in the study were often found among those who were socially disadvantaged. And they found that people who scored high on an index of devotionalism were *most* likely to favor civil rights and to accept the unacceptable in society.

What has happened to these "weak" people who are devout? Their devotion to God has given them strength that they could not obtain in the world. Paul knew this power of God as a strength for those who are despised by the world. He honored those who are weak in the eyes of the world because they are strong in the Lord. Because of this strength, he can also admonish them to honor those who are "strong" in the eyes of the world. If the "weak" really place God's honor first, then they can live in harmony with those who are strong. The observing of feasts or festivals, church attendance and duties will not dishonor the strong in the eyes of the weak or the weak in the eyes of the strong, for each of them obtains his or her ultimate strength from a power far beyond his or her human capabilities.

This devotional dimension of faith gives a new definition of strong and weak. As Paul wrote in 1 Corinthians, God gives strength to those who are weak in the eyes of the world in order that we may see the true source of strength for all people (1:21ff.). In this, Paul follows the example of Christ who consistently acted as a servant among those who called him Lord and called upon his disciples to do the same.

Is it realistic for a pastor to ask the weak to honor the strong? Do the strong actually make a Christian contribution in the church? A survey on Spencer County, Indiana, churches showed that new ideas in society and religion were accepted by young adults and professional people, those with extremely low and extremely high incomes, and those with a high-school education and above.[6] The "strong" are more open to change. These are the persons who expect the church to maintain an adequate program of Christian education and worship and to work for justice even when this threatens traditional attitudes.[7]

A Design for Functioning Together Faithfully

A shepherd can provide a design by which the strong will work with the weak toward Christian objectives that may threaten individual security. This requires as much patience and understanding from adequate people as it requires courage from the inadequate. Paul ought to reduce the contempt and impatience of the former by writing: "We who are strong ought to bear with the failings of the weak, and not to please ourselves; let each of us please his neighbor for his good, to edify him" (Rom. 15:1–2).

The design for commitment despite diversity is to identify the strengths of the weak and the weaknesses of the strong, to build up both the weak and the strong through their Christian commitment. Mutual participation in the Christian fellowship, despite the awareness of diversity, is a daily school of Christian discipleship, in which each teaches the other.

Let's suppose that Jim shows growing enthusiasm for shepherding skills that will bring the strong and the weak together in an organization. If he's realistic, he'll then ask, "But how can I manage this by myself? I want this to happen, but I can't counsel every member about his or her strengths and weaknesses!"

To answer this question is to show how a concern for people will be most effective and enduring when we utilize organizational principles. There are at least three ongoing procedures that will increase the faithful functioning of the weak and the strong with one another in the church: (1) the coordination of plans, (2) a standardization of practices, and (3) mutual adjustment. Each of these elements of faithfulness will reassure the weak that they know where they are going—toward godly purposes—and encourage the strong to build with trust and faith.

1. The coordination of plans is a recognition that differences between people have been faced and a workable covenant has been agreed upon for the implementation of common purposes.

Jim has already been faithful in this function as he planned for the retirement of the music director. He has worked with the church's committees that were responsible for decisions about the music program, and he has seen that the policies concerning hiring and firing were followed with impartiality.

This trustworthiness in policies and procedures is basic to any activity that a pastor may pursue in administration. It is a sign that the shepherd cares for his people. In turn, they can place their confidence in the pastor. This is so important to most church leaders that it was among the top three expectations of laypeople of their pastors in the nationwide study "Readiness for Ministry." Lay leaders said they expected their pastor to be someone who would carry out staff and church decisions without regard for recognition and with consistency despite opposition.

2. The second sign of faithfulness to both the weak and the strong is the standardization of actions. As we have just seen in the category presented by laypeople to the ideal pastor, a leader is expected to stand by decisions. This means that the leader is realistic in the assessment of what has been done right and what has been done wrong, and by whom. The faithful leader does not project

failure upon others when the difficulty lies with the leadership.

When decisions are made through compromise or the pressure of special interest, then a pastor is vulnerable to the kind of criticisms that are now being made of Jim by the relatives of the ousted music director. They accuse him of improper methods of administration. The pastor's security will lie in an ability to describe the regularity of procedures. In this way, those who love the music director will see that justice has been done. They may still favor the music director over any other person for the position, but they cannot realistically accuse the church of injustice.

At times, it may appear that the use of standardized procedures is cumbersome and inhibits change. This is always a problem that must be faced in an institution. But at the same time, the changes must be made in a way that is agreed upon by all the people who are concerned about the change; and, before changes are made, the people must establish trust in the leadership as they see that decisions are faithfully carried out according to the procedures that are agreed upon. In this way, the faithfulness of the leaders becomes a basis for the trust of others in the possibility of change.

If there is a track record of trust (which is usually built up through a variety of pastoral contacts), then changes can take place without loss of faith in the leadership. This is especially important with the dependent people who often insist upon rigid implementation of policies and strict adherence to procedures. Such people dread change as a "rocking of the ark."

3. One of the most difficult issues in administration is the difference between the "weak" and the "strong" concerning compromises. On the one hand, the weak are cautious of any changes that would threaten their organizational security. On the other hand, the strong are very impatient with the insistence of the weak upon bureaucratic details concerning the static nature of an organization. And they accuse the weak of cowardice in relation to new and untried programs.

This is a time for pastors to honor the differences between people, without subverting the larger goals of the church. Pastors must call upon the reservoir of trust that they have built up with the weak to give them confidence in new programs that require faith that the weak do not have. Pastors must also point to their courage and spirit of adventure in talking with the strong, so that occasional compromises and adjustments in new programs will not appear to be a lack of faith for the future.

This kind of pastoral challenge could be very appealing to Jim, for it demonstrates the way in which Christian maturity can come to people of very different psychological and spiritual backgrounds. It is a consistent emphasis of successful pastors. Washington Gladden wrote at the turn of the twentieth century, in *A Christian Pastor in the Working Church*, that much of his success with reactionary members of the congregation came because of their personal faith in him as their minister in time of trouble. Because they believed in him, they would accept new emphasis upon the social gospel that was completely at variance with their narrow definition of the church as an agency only for the salvation of individual souls. The same emphasis came out of the investigations of eight changing Presbyterian churches by Grace Goodman, who found that long-term trust in some Sunday school teacher, elder, or pastor was the major factor in the church's turning toward the relevant needs of transitional neighborhoods. When a trusted leader called for change, the people were willing to follow.

The Controlling Emotion: Love

The apostle Paul stressed the essential factor of faithfulness when he founded leadership upon the "root and ground of love" (Eph. 3:17). Love enhances both the devotional emphasis upon our faithfulness to Christ and the pastoral emphasis of our confidence in a trusted leader. And a pastor certainly finds basic satisfaction in the increase of love between members of the congregation.

How does the pastor's emphasis upon love alter the attitudes and actions of both dependent and independent people concerning programs at the church?

There are two parts to my answer. One depends on an inner, psychological process, the development of power in "the inner man" (Eph. 3:16). With this personal integrity, people do not need to be so completely dependent upon the opinions of others, or defend themselves so quickly, or be on guard against attack. There can be more openness to those who are independent, who were formerly thought of as dangers to institutional security. The independent can also be more open in their frustrations with those who are dependent and come to some recognition of the strengths of the dependent persons in terms of dependability and carefulness. In this way, perfect love can cast out mutual fear and contempt (1 John 4:18).

The other devotional development is more communal or administrative. It is found in the loving character of the community upon which people depend. Many of the socially deprived people in the studies of Glock and Campbell were seeking a substitute family in the church. This is a legitimate function of a supportive organization. But will they expect the same of the church as they did of their family? Will they act toward church members as they did toward mother and father, brother and sister, son or daughter? This is a difficult question, since many of the expectations of a family are not the same as that which we would expect of people who are related in Christian love. The weak may transfer expectations and ways of relating from family to church without change; and the church will then be saturated with sibling rivalries, resentment of parents, dependency upon powerful figures, and reaction to dominance that are so characteristic of those who are dependent. (If Jim has some training in marriage and family counseling, he'll be more sensitive to the characteristics that configure an affirmative versus a conflicting family.)

The reaction of the strong to this emphasis upon the family of God's church may be disgust when they see how the weak understand personal relationships. The temptation of independent people is then to withdraw from active leadership and to despise those who act in the church as they would at home.

The challenge to the strong is to work with the weak to see new relationships of love in God's family. When independent people are recruited for leadership, they can lead groups in which people talk about what they expect of others and how they have related to other members of the congregation. Dependent people will be especially influenced by these conversations if the independent leaders recognize the importance of dependence upon others. Both the strong and the weak can then find an ideal in the balance between self-regulation and sensitivity to the needs of others.[8]

An Application

Would Jim be "turned on" by this challenge of church management? Yes, if we accept his manifest desire to be a counselor of troubled people. For much counseling by pastors will entail conflict management, the resentment of a "weak" spouse and the frustration felt by a "strong" spouse. Or there will be continual calls for arbitration and clarification of disputes between an assertive child and a controlling parent. If Jim enjoys the results of these consultations, he can also find fulfillment in adjustments between the strong and the weak in the organizational life of the church.

Here is an illustration of a direct crossover from pastoral counseling to church management in my conversations with my lay moderator of the congregation about the strong and the weak:

LARRY: Preacher, do you think I am too pushy? I don't mean to order people around in the church—like I can do in my company— but I want us to get things done.

PASTOR: Larry, what you're doing is essential to leadership. You set goals with others and pursue them faithfully. The problem is with your power. You have it whether you're in this office or in a church council.

LARRY: Now wait a minute. I don't want to run things at the church. I'm glad for others to be in leadership. And I surely don't want the spotlight. Maybe I should back up, not accept the moderator position [the church had just elected him moderator for a second year]. But then I've always wanted to see things done, organize them. If I'm offered a job to do that, I accept it. But I think others should have responsibilities and honors also.

PASTOR: Good. I tell people that they'll just have to have the courage to say "stop" when you're moving too fast. You may still push, but you will listen to them. And that's something I want to ask. Why do you keep on working when someone opposes your plans? Why don't you stop to "get" the one who annoys you?

LARRY: That wouldn't do any good. We've got a job to do in the church. I don't like being sidetracked, but it's really not my ball game anyway. It's the Lord's work. Why should I fuss if another Christian sees things differently? What gets me is the person who won't say what he thinks or who holds something against me for years. Why do some people do that?

PASTOR: Because you represent power and they feel put down. They think of church decisions as win or lose, you're up and they're down.

LARRY: I don't see why they think that way. I enjoy seeing things getting done, but I don't have to get the credit.

PASTOR: Why not?

LARRY: It's not right to think that way. We're supposed to glorify God in the church. We're his servants, and we should not be proud of ourselves.

PASTOR: But you are proud of yourself in some ways.

LARRY: Well, yes, I've done well in the world [pause]. Maybe that's why I'm willing to share the credit in the church. But why can't I get this across to others? They don't hear me say, 'I suggest.' They just hear what I say as *the* word—or at least some of them do [smiles].

On the following Sunday afternoon, Larry gave the church council some examples of his "pushing to get things done." He said that some of them got angry with him because of it and he wanted to know how things were now. Several members agreed that his examples were relevant, that he did persist in one course, but they had learned or were learning to give their reasons for alternative courses of actions when they saw one.

These conversations illustrate the importance of an adorable and compelling object of faith. The leadership's attention must be focused on purposes beyond their own security or anxiety, which reduces their dogmatism and anesthetizes them to small jabs at their self-esteem.

Love Can Balance Dependence and Independence

The controlling emotion of love for Christ will balance dependence and independence in several ways.

1. All Christians can share a vision of God, even though some have trouble making up their minds about some moral or administrative choices that are presented to them. There will always be divisions because some people can make decisions and others hesitate. That which brings the shy and the confident members together is a divine personality, a model that all seek to follow. Some church members might be provoked by Larry's swift decisions, but they can agree with him in service to and judgment by the same Lord. A leader needs character as well as decisiveness.

2. The character of the leaders is measured not only by a vision of God but also by a steady picture of self and others. A realistic assessment of people and places is necessary for independent leaders to get along with and bring along the dependent members of a group. Larry could see that some of his words in church were magnified by his secular position. He noted people's inability to interpret him as he tried to communicate. He also knew something about himself, that satisfaction and recognition in his job prevented him from being hungry for praise in the church.

To be "rooted and grounded in love" is literally to have your feet on the ground, to know what is going on.

3. No leader has a complete picture of what is going on in a group, himself, or others. We can never be completely sure of ourselves. Larry asks questions about himself and about his incomplete communications. Then he affirms his belief that the glory of God is to be the chief aim of every church member. He does not retreat from the pain of self-criticism by speaking of his own glory and his own accomplishments. He's proud of these, but he does not meet God's ideal. He continues to know it only in part.

An independent person may seem so sure of himself in the presence of those who hesitate that there is a temptation to become dogmatic. It seems reasonable to allay the uncertainties of the weak through a leader's reassuring confidence. But dogmatism increases the powerlessness of the weak and the tendency toward manipulation by the strong. The antidote for this dogmatism is a humble awareness of our partial knowledge and our selfish motivation. When Paul wrote: "Let him who boasts, boast of the Lord" (1 Cor. 1:31), he was providing a necessary balance for the strong among the weak.

4. God's love allows dependent and independent people to live with each other's differences. I kept reinforcing Larry's awareness of his sureness and the contrast with others' insecurity. Some of them were measuring every situation by who won or lost, while he kept moving toward objective goals that had little to do with personal recognition. Larry wanted to recognize something in himself, to be satisfied with his accomplishments. He must learn that many church people live instead by the way others judge them. They depend more on his recognition and the pastor's recognition than they do on their own.

When a leader can respect dependent people, even though their ways of thinking are different, they can work together. What happens when a leader gives others the security of accepting them in spite of their differences from him? This encourages in dependent people a corresponding type of affection. They are led by Christ's love to allow independent people a separate existence without envy or a desire to bring them down. Each person can have his or her own psychological "space." With this security, each can be hospitable to the "stranger" who is either weak or strong.

LUECKE

To Build the Body as an Architect

Sam's friend Jim has the characteristics of a task-oriented leader. He spends most of his time thinking about things to do at the church. The administrative role of pastor seems to come naturally. He is quite ready to tend to the committees, be in charge, and "keep a steady helm."

Yet, this pastor is in a leadership crisis. It is not that the church is rejecting his leadership. His administrative instincts were intact when he lined up the key supporters before taking action with the minister of music. Rather, he finds himself a leader who has run out of administrative vision. He is burned out.

Burnout happens to many pastors. What used to be a joy becomes a burden. Where they used to see opportunities, they now see demands. The demands start picking them apart. Because others' expectations are so constant in it, the administrative role is the dimension of ministry most readily associated with burnout.

The best thing about this situation is that Jim is not yet ready to settle into a maintenance mode of pastoral leadership. This is a common resolution for leaders who can reconcile themselves just to coping with the operations that are in place. This pastor would rather think about a new personal challenge, such as a full-time counselor, than trudge along in the routines he has mastered. He seems to be a builder at heart. Put in the best light, if he does not see any more church programs to build, he would rather concentrate on building up people individually.

The choice between programs or people is, of course, an artificial one. The two can be the same building effort. Jim's perception of his quandary may have several explanations. One is a narrow concept of the task of administrative leadership. Another is a temporary depression that is clouding his whole view of life. If Jim is depressed, in a clinical sense, his interest in becoming a counselor could really be a request for help from a counselor.

The relation between perception of task and emotional well-being is no simple matter. Each can affect the other. For leaders who feel burned out, a sensitive, supportive colleague can help air feelings and bring some relief. Another approach is to focus on the task perception. Changing the concept of the leadership task is one way pastors can recover energy and enthusiasm for their administrative work.

The building vision of administration is basic to staying fresh. Building is inherently more fun than maintaining. It seems to me that doing administrative work without a vision of developing something different and better is bound to be dreary. In describing his pastoral leadership, the apostle Paul gives us clear theological linkages between ministry and the changing work of building.

There are several kinds of builders. I find it helpful to distinguish between carpenters, contractors, and architects. St. Paul thought of himself as an architect. While pastors usually have to function as carpenters and contractors in their congregation, they will get the most enjoyment out of their work if they approach it as an architect.

Jim seems to be operating a contractor ministry and not enjoying it. He is hoping a specialized carpentry ministry of counseling will bring relief. He should try the challenge of an architectural ministry. It offers the greatest potential for the people-oriented ministry. It is the best insurance against administrative burnout.

Three Types of Builder

The apostle Paul relied heavily on the building analogy to explain ministry in a congregation. The verb *oiko-domeo* appears twenty-eight times in his writing. Literally, it means "to make a house." Often, it is translated weakly as "to edify." When Paul talks about building or edifying, we should imagine people constructing a house.

Picture a house under construction today. What kind of builders work on it, and what are their roles? The easiest to envision are the hands-on builders. These are the carpenters, plumbers, electricians, and so on—the workers who change the wood, pipes, or wire from raw material into functional components. Usually, carpenters are the most visible and make the most dramatic changes.

I like to see carpenters as the representative trade for hands-on builders. Jesus himself was a carpenter. As a tentmaker by trade, Paul certainly understood hands-on construction. But in his ministry, he seemed to have more stable structures in mind, for he did not make much use of the tent analogy. Scripturally, we could choose a bricklayer as the representative trade. This fits in with

Peter's building analogy of God's people as "living stone, . . . built into a spiritual house," with Christ as the cornerstone (1 Pet. 2:4–6). But building technology has changed, and Jesus' trade is more basic today.

The change in technology brought another kind of builder to the forefront. This is the contractor. His role is to get the right kind of workers and the appropriate materials together in an orderly, timely fashion within available financial resources. Contractors became more important as houses got more complicated to build. When they were simply walls and a roof, a carpenter could get the job done reasonably well by himself. Building became a different matter when heating systems, bathrooms, electrical appliances, and other modern necessities appeared. As hands-on building became more specialized and the choice of material more difficult, getting everything ready for building became a skill of its own.

The contractor and the workers do not make up the whole team. They depend on the contribution of an architect, the third kind of builder. The architect provides the design for how the size and configuration of the rooms will fit the functions that will go on within them and also for how the house will fit the chosen site. The architect's work results in the drawn plans or blueprints that guide the total effort.

St. Paul appreciated the key role of the architect. He was willing to assume that responsibility himself. In the building analogy presented in 1 Corinthians 3:10–17, the self-description of his role is usually translated as master builder. But architect is the word in the original text. He set the foundation or determined the basic design. Others built on it.

A pastor today can ask whether he or she functions as a carpenter, a contractor, or an architect. This question assumes the pastor thinks like a builder and is not willing to settle for a maintenance role, repairing the same leaks or sweeping the same floors over and over again.

Carpenter ministry. Much of ministry amounts to carpentry. Preaching, teaching, leading worship, counseling, evangelizing, providing pastoral care—these are the basic ministry functions that can change people spiritually. If the pastor assumes responsibility personally to provide these direct, hands-on building services, it is a carpentry ministry. Sometimes, it is done with the assistance of a few carpenter's helpers.

Carpenter ministry is essential. It remains the basic function of pastoral ministry. Most ministers also derive much of their professional satisfaction from one or the other specialty. They can see what has to be done and do it competently without a lot of fuss and bother. Within their specialty, they can get results. Such satisfaction is certainly attractive.

The difficulty with ministry at the hands-on level is that progress is slow and the building stays simple. A carpenter can only do so much in a day. Only the rare carpenter can do all the building tasks equally well. Meanwhile, the church does not hold still, and the carpenter diverts more and more time to patching up what is falling apart. Carpenter ministers do best in small churches or specialized ministries. They have to adjust their leadership vision accordingly.

Contractor ministry. Contractor ministry begins with the realization that God's people are not just the raw material, the stones to be built together by the pastor. Rather, they can be bricklayers, plumbers, or carpenters themselves—lively stones supporting and changing each other. They, too, can exhort, teach, witness, counsel, and care for each other. Then the central task is to coordinate all of their ministries. This involves recruiting members into their specialized building role, helping them each understand their tasks, getting them together with the people who are their "raw material," scheduling their separate efforts, settling disputes, and somehow assuring that the whole enterprise does what it is supposed to do.

Contractor ministry is administration. Carpenters have little need for administrator skills; they do the work themselves. Contractors depend on others to get the work done. Accomplishing goals through others is a basic definition of management. The contractor emerged as a key role when house-building technology got complicated. The pastoral administrative role becomes more important when the theology of church life emphasizes the involvement of the laity in ministry.

Contractor ministry can be exciting. With its underlying theology, it can tap tremendous energy for the life and growth of the church. But like carpentry, contractor ministry has its limitations. Administrative work can get so focused on diverse details that the activity it guides does not add up to a building. Or what the lead builders can make is not a house that meets the needs of the members. Or the house the workers like remains a human habitation with little room for the God who called that church into existence in the first place.

Contractors need a design, and they get it from someone else.

If the design is not right, the building effort does not achieve its purpose. Then a contractor emphasis can turn ministry into a frustrating job that feels like a never-ending waste of time. When the house under construction does not seem to fit together right, everyone loses interest. Finding workers is difficult. Meetings become boring. Members feel used. Conflict abounds. Everything is harder. Progress is slow. Burnout looms on the horizon.

One pastoral response to administrative work when it becomes a hassle is to give up being a contractor. Carpentry looks more attractive. But another response is to pay more attention to the design. This is architectural ministry.

The Challenge of Architectural Ministry

I learned the value of an architect's contribution firsthand with a house-building project of my own. When our family grew by another child, we wanted to build a bedroom addition. I knew where the room should go and roughly how to tie it in with the rest of the house. But I could not resolve the design for some of the specifics, like the roof line and window configuration. I was particularly stumped by how to get light into the rest of the house once a key exterior window became an interior doorway.

Finally, I gave in and engaged the services of an experienced architect. He listened to my hopes and problems. He spent several hours walking around the yard, reflecting on the existing structure and its possibilities. A week later, he presented a design that was unlike anything I had ever envisioned on my own. A little vestibule with a skylight solved the lighting problem. Windows and roof lines were graceful and exciting, yet simple. What could have been a boxy, obvious add-on became a structure of beauty that integrated a previous addition and completed a corner of the house. I then was able to work out the details of the design, to contract for the rough framing, and to do the finish carpentry myself. I still look back with pride on that project.

Architects bring three kinds of contributions to building. The most basic is the ability to envision what the outcome should look like and to make structural sense out of all the possible components and relationships. This is the most creative part of the whole building process. Everything else, for better or worse, depends on the overall design. It is like laying the foundation, as St. Paul describes it.

After the overall design emerges, architects produce the detailed construction documents that guide the contractor and the workers. This is the most evident contribution during the project. The blueprints specify door and window sizes, the location of electrical outlets, the layout of plumbing fixtures, and so on. This contribution is less creative. But good blueprints significantly reduce building confusion and frustration later.

The other contribution actually precedes the point of creative design. Architects need to understand what purposes the building will serve, as well as the distinctive features of its intended site. The good architects spend a lot of time listening to the people who will use it. They help sort out the priorities for the needs to be met, both functionally and aesthetically. Then the design can emerge as a coherent and fitting response.

If this is what architects do, what would architectural ministry be? The equivalent of physical space in a building would be the activities of the people gathered as a congregation. Getting a focus for diverse activities is like placing walls to define space. Providing for coordination is like arranging rooms for convenient movement from one to the other. Architectural ministry in a congregation is the shaping of programs that structure the sharing relationships of the members.

An architect envisions a building outcome with drawings for reaction before it is built. The one who helped me with my house addition even made a three-dimensional cardboard model so I could see what it would look like. Congregational architects would envision activity outcomes in terms of how many people are doing what kinds of activity how often and in what setting. What could the worship life look like? The educational life? The witnessing life and service life? The design lays out how to achieve such outcomes.

Ministry of this sort can happen only when there is a vision of a different and better future. The energy to build springs from dreams. Designers give shape to the vision. But they have to listen and observe carefully to be sure that the vision is shared by those who are going to participate. Architectural ministry cannot be dictatorial. It is responsive. Stimulating vision through encounters with God and his word is certainly central to such a ministry, as is refining it through shared discussion. The special architectural challenge is to temper the vision with reality, so that the intended outcome is something that a particular congregation can actually accomplish with the resources they have.

Too often, the design for congregational life is simply inherited and assumed. Churches have a Sunday morning worship service and Sunday school classes, which follow a pretty standard routine. Members divide up for specialized activities in a choir and some service groups. Evangelism and education committees, and a few others, complete the "rooms" of the house. The leaders then try to think up things to do to keep the participants busy. When the basic design has lost its vision and is left unexamined, the church leadership cannot help but be mostly carpenter and contractor ministries. The architectural interest left is mostly tinkering with the blueprint.

This building analogy is a way of describing the development of organization in a congregation. In the previous chapter, I summarized several models or theories of church organization. One is the classical model that tries to prescribe ideal specialized responsibilities and duties for the various workers. Leaders then try to fit people into that structure. This model often produces an uninteresting and unsatisfying design because it is done without careful observation of the interests and needs of the specific gathered people who are going to live in the house. Designing with mechanistic bureaucratic thinking easily overlooks the responsive dimension of architectural ministry. It often also does not get around to recognizing a vision. Besides, once the structure is laid out on paper, the fun of creative design is too quickly over.

Human relations thinking is another model. It stresses widespread participation in developing a vision. Listening is highly refined through continuous discussions. The difficulty is that the process does not emphasize a "master builder," an architect who will pull all of the dreams together into an integrated design. The working plans tend to remain sketchy, too. Actually, there are usually dozens of plans floating around, many of which are not realistic. Because results so often are secondary to the process, progress is slow. Leader burnout happens frequently.

Architectural ministry contributes the most and is the most rewarding in the context of systems thinking about church organization.

Architectural Design for God's Garden

As described in the previous chapter, systems theory draws on organic analogies more than mechanical ones, although both have their place. In his architectural ministry, Paul could shift his thinking from one to the other quickly. He states his identity as an architect in 1 Corinthians 3:10 and goes on to talk about how others should carefully put the material together on his foundation. But in the verses just before this, he was thinking about himself as someone who plants a church, which others water—God gives the growth. Verse 9 puts the two analogies side by side: You (the church in Corinth) are God's garden, God's house.

Paul's conceptual dexterity calls for a similar dexterity in naming the designer's role for congregational life. For God's garden, such a leader would be a master gardener, just as there should be a master builder when thinking about God's house. Taking a little liberty, I will merge concepts and talk about organic architecture. Landscape architecture is a more conventional term. By whatever description, I am talking about the most comprehensive understanding of the administrative role of pastor.

Designing with an emphasis on organic systems thinking recognizes that, once started, a congregation does have a life of its own with many interdependent components. As with any living organism, change will occur as people and relationships go through cycles of growth and decline. Carpenters and contractors are inclined to resist all but the most carefully planned changes that happen on their terms. Organic designers welcome change. They count on it as the reason for their contribution. Without springtime and fall, growth in some areas and decline in others, God's garden would not be a very interesting place. His involvement in the life of his people would be hard to see.

Jim, the burned-out pastor at the beginning, thought like a contractor builder. He wanted to reduce congregational change to what his blueprints called for. The effort was exhausting, and he was too tired to change the plan. If he would think more like an organic architect, he could relax and enjoy the divergent interests and scattered conflict in the congregation. There is life in this garden. He has something to work with and respond to. There is a source of ever-refreshing vitality right in front of him.

The pastoral task is to provide ever-adaptive leadership that makes sense out of all the potential growth within the system of interaction that is the church community. In systems theory, administrative leadership revolves around continually clarifying purposes and interpreting how participants can fit their interests and activities into achieving these purposes. Understanding existing and potential interdependencies is necessary preparation. Describing purposes as a vision that most participants can share is the design work that becomes the leader's most creative contribution. Interpretation involves helping the participants to compare current activity that is becoming ineffective to what could be done better. When the vision is compelling (like an appealing house design), the participants will be more inclined to channel their energy in that direction.

For month-by-month working plans, this kind of architectural ministry oversees the fertilizing and pruning processes of congregational life. Where the participants have worship, educational, witnessing, or service interests that make sense in the overall vision, the master gardener encourages the organization to provide appropriate water and fertilizer to help their efforts grow. Where activities will divert energy and produce weeds that do not contribute to the vision, this kind of administrator encourages steps that will prune where it is appropriate. Pastor Jim took such steps with his minister of music, who was "retired." Perhaps Jim had good design reasons. It would be interesting to know whether this participant presented interests that could have been cultivated within an overall vision, or whether there was simply a contractor dispute over working conditions.

In his organic architect's role, St. Paul saw himself planting a church and cultivating its life. But he did not presume to make or even choose the seeds. God does this. More specifically, Paul had a keen sense of the Holy Spirit's workings among God's people, giving seeds of vitality for the common good. His teachings about the gifts of the Spirit interpret the starting point for the wonderfully diverse growth and change that can happen in the system of a church's interaction.

Carpenter leaders see themselves as the workers in a church. Contractor leaders try to recruit members into worker roles. Pastors who are ready to be organic architects find themselves in a field full of workers, at least in seed form. "To each is given the manifestation of the Spirit for the common good" (1 Cor. 12:7). All this kind of builder has to do is to recognize their individual, potential contributions as seed gifts from God and then to get them planted where they will do the most good.

This organic perspective makes a highly significant difference for church administration. Instead of thinking up programs that need workers, a gardener/administrator can concentrate on supporting workers in need of program guidance. Instead of fitting people to the plan, leaders fit the plan to the people wherever possible.

Change is managed rather than resisted. Somewhere, the church always has energy that can be tapped and channeled.

With this perspective, the design for congregational life is never fixed for all time. It continually unfolds as God gives gifts of new healers, helpers, teachers, financial contributors, musicians, and specialized administrators—people with new interests and abilities who are ready to be cultivated and integrated into the vision that pulls the body of Christ together. The vision itself keeps evolving because the Holy Spirit keeps working through the congregational prophets, preachers, and exhorters who can see needs and make causes come alive for others. The creative tension between the diversity and unity of these bodily organs, the balance for these moving parts, keeps shifting as various leaders exercise wisdom and knowledge to assess the health of the body.

The appointed pastor is only one of these God-given workers. Maybe he or she is not the one most gifted to be the overall architect who can guide all the budding activity in a coherent, purposeful direction. But the pastor is in the best position to try. A church garden turns into a beautiful, life-affirming house when there is such administrative leadership.

God promises insight and strength to the ministers he calls as organic architects. Those who are willing to follow the lead of the Holy Spirit are in for a tremendously exciting time.

Top-Level Church Management

Systems theory is especially helpful for thinking about church life with its unique spiritual dynamics. But this perspective is general enough to be applied to a wide range of organizations. It is taught and pursued especially among upper-level managers of corporations. As organizations grow, presidents and vice-presidents function increasingly as designers of organizational performance. Their work is often called strategic management. Middle managers operate within the design laid out higher up, and they function mostly as contractors. All of these managers are a step or two removed from the people who do the actual work.

One reason pastors often find church administration unrewarding is that they do not know how to think like top-level managers. This may be because they do not think like managers at all; they try to do all the work themselves. Or it may be that they associate administration with the work of first- and middle-level managers. After all, most professional managers that a pastor would meet operate at these levels of limited scope. The top level has the most freedom for creative design. Pastors can do organizational ministry at this level if they want. The benefits for church life can be great. Architectural ministers have plenty of opportunity for "kicks" along the way.

Summary

Our case of the "Burned-Out Pastor" was chosen so that each of us could see glimmers of his own leadership instincts in a pastor who has run out of steam for his ministry of administration. We approached it as if, in turn, Southard and Luecke sat down with Jim in his study to offer some words of encouragement. Each said: Look at it this way. With the interests that seem to turn you on, you can keep your administrative work exciting if you take this view of how to get at it.

For pastors who are naturally support oriented, Southard appeals to a self-identity as a counselor. He holds forth the New Testament theme of helping the weak and the strong reconcile their differences. It takes a counselor's instincts to identify and honor both the weak and the strong. Southard shows how the routine administrative work of coordinating plans, standardizing actions, and finding compromises becomes an extension of a counselor's concern for increasing the respect people show each other. A pastor can find excitement in heading a daily school of Christian discipline. Southard urges that even in administration pastors learn to see and emphasize love as the controlling emotion that can alter the attitudes and actions of both dependent and independent people in church programs.

For pastors who are naturally task oriented, Luecke appeals to a self-identity as a builder. He holds forth the Pauline theme of building the body of Christ. Many pastors approach their tasks like a hands-on builder, such as a carpenter, but then discover the frustrations of how little they can personally do in a church and how much of their own energy it takes. If they see the task as getting the body built up, they will see more progress when they learn to function as a contractor. The design work of an architect allows the most scope for continued creativity and fresh insights in a body-building task that is always evolving in new ways. Luecke urges pastors to try to think like top-level managers of strategy, instead of middle-level or supervisory managers.

5

How Administrators Can "Move" People

The Cluster Volunteers

"How are we going to get our cluster leaders to do their job better?" This was the question the pastor and committee members were tussling with in their monthly meeting at Our Shepherd Church. Rev. Diane Proctor was with four members of the fellowship committee. They were reviewing progress in their cluster program.

"That's the trouble with church work," said Tom, one of the committee. "You have to depend on volunteers. There isn't much you can do if they don't follow through with their assignment. We couldn't run things that way where I work."

Pastor Proctor often had the same thoughts, although she was careful not to express them among her people. With fellow pastors, though, the problem of volunteer workers was a frequent topic of conversation. They assured each other there was not much to learn from management practices because, after all, they have to depend on volunteers, not paid workers.

The cluster program grew out of discussions which Pastor Proctor started soon after she came to Our Shepherd three years ago. She discovered others in the church who shared her concern that a number of individuals and families were not actively involved in the fellowship life of the church. The fellowship committee evolved out of those early discussions. The committee members, including Pastor Proctor, were excited about the potential that small groups have for drawing people closer together and helping them care for each other.

Their plan seemed reasonable when they launched the cluster program two years ago. With the approval of the elders, they divided the church membership up into clusters of about fifteen to twenty adults, considering a number of factors but mostly geography. Within each cluster, they recruited one person to serve as the leader. Each leader was supposed to bring the cluster together several times a year in a home for a shared activity like a potluck or Bible study. The leader was also supposed to "shepherd" the cluster members to the extent of keeping track of illnesses and other needs for which support could be provided.

The first year, almost all the clusters did meet at least once, and most of them met a second time. But this last year, only five of the fourteen clusters seemed to be doing much of anything. These were led by members of this planning committee. Pastor Proctor knew, too, that she was receiving little help with pastoral care from the other cluster leaders.

The frustration in this evening committee meeting was high. There was some sentiment toward dropping the program. But no one was really serious about giving up. The idea was too good, and they all believed that something should be done to improve the fellowship life of the church. They kept coming back to the cluster leaders as the crux of the problem. They wanted to find some way to help them pay more attention to their groups.

"Why do people volunteer and then not follow through with their promise?" wondered Alice, one of the most active leaders. "Maybe we need to talk more about Christian commitment in the church."

<u>**LUECKE**</u>

Selecting, Training, and Motivating "Volunteers"

How to "move" people is a constant concern for pastors. Much of preaching is intended to help Christians move to a fuller, more life-transforming faith or to a greater love for others. In one-to-one counseling, pastors try to help individuals move into greater self-understanding in Christ and more effective relationships with family.

The administrative function of pastoring makes the concern for movement most apparent. It emphasizes the doing of specific activities and tasks within the church. Whether or not this happens can be seen by those who care to look. For this reason, program development can be hazardous for church leaders. It necessitates dependence on the movement of others. Such dependence opens up the possibility of evident failure.

Pastor Proctor and her committee colleagues were looking at a program failure, and it did not feel good. A few more experiences like this, and she will probably register high on the list of pastors who complain about church administration as a real drag in the pastorate. Behind much pastoral frustration with administration are experiences of setting out a course of action and finding that few members stir themselves up to move that way.

Whatever her natural tendencies, Pastor Proctor was clearly in a task-oriented mode of leadership with this cluster program. She as well as others on the committee were looking at people not as they are but as they could become. Support was their underlying concern. But support had become a task for others to do. Southard discusses how the pastor might have pursued support with a supportive style of leadership. I see it as a situation where there is a goal that is ahead of most of the people. Leaders are looking for ways to move them toward that specific, known goal. This is a common and appropriate situation that belongs in the area of shaping a church covenant for the journey, as presented in chapter 2.

Moving people toward the accomplishment of known goals is at the heart of the modern practice of management. Pastor Proctor can be excused for thinking that management has little to offer pastors. She shares with others a faulty understanding of it. True, leadership is usually labeled management in a context where workers are paid. Yet, giving people money is but one way to get them to do something. It is hardly the only way recognized and practiced by managers. In dealing with unpaid volunteers, the options are narrowed. But the overall personnel framework of a management approach still has much to commend it in settings like Our Shepherd Church.

I would like to sketch out how the personnel framework could be applied to help pastoral administrators "move" volunteer church workers in programmed effort. The most relevant category is motivation. Selection also has to be considered; so does training. These are basic functions of managing people. Pastors are right when they resist simply adopting common management practices in these areas. The appeal to work in the church has to flow from spiritual dynamics. But this starting point does not alter the need to pay attention to selection, training, and the context for personal motivation of church volunteers.

The Push and Pull of Leading Christians into Action

The writer of Hebrews offers a succinct biblical formulation for the problem of leading volunteers: "Let us consider how to stir up one another to love and good works" (10:24). The next verse presents the oft-quoted admonition against neglect to meet together so that such encouragement can be provided. Basic to congregational life is motivating one another to actions of Christian love.

Accepting the invitation to consider how to do this, we can look at the effort to engage individual Christians in specified action as a push-pull process. Participants in church programs are there because they feel something internally pushing them into action expressive of their life in Christ. The specific form of action they take on a given day happens because of a pull exerted by others around them.

The decision to volunteer as a Sunday school teacher, for instance, will not happen without a person's desire to reach out and teach others. This is an internal push, wherever it comes from. The person will not wind up as a faithful Sunday school staff member, though, without someone else showing him or her where a teacher is needed and how the staff works together in the program. This is the external pull. To pull does not necessarily mean to apply unwelcome force. It is to provide a concrete opportunity that attracts and channels general movement, much like a metal object can pull an energized magnet toward it.

Church leaders have to concern themselves with both the push and the pull. An emphasis on one without the other will hamper the joining together of believers into God's household, to use the building analogy pursued in the previous chapter. The push of faith without the application to works is dead (James 2:26). But church work that pulls without the push of faith among participants will also die.

The preacher rôle and the administrator role of a pastor are quite different, in part, because each stresses a different emphasis in the push-pull process of motivation. As a preacher, the pastor stresses the push of God's word enlivening hearers through the Spirit. As an administrator, the pastor stresses the offering of specific opportunities that can pull believers into concrete expressions of their response to the Spirit's push.

We are concentrating here on the administrator role. In the limited focus of this role, the pastor also has limited ability to move people. All she or he can do is try to make opportunities for action as attractive as possible. If others do not respond, it is either because they did not feel much of an internal push in that direction or they do not see how the specific opportunity addresses what they want to do. Decisions about their action rest within the individuals. Administrators can only arrange the context for their decision making.

My use of a push-pull distinction is an attempt to develop for church application an assumption that is almost a truism in management theory on motivation. Strictly speaking, managers cannot motivate anyone. All they can do is respond more effectively to the motives or movement they recognize in others. The administrative challenge is to understand the various individual motives and figure out what context will best help those people stay in motion toward goals that are agreeable to both the manager and the people. Some of the major theorists associated with this sort of view are Douglas McGregor, Frederich Herzberg, Rensis Likert, and Chris Argyris. The current summary is called the expectancy theory of motivation or path-goals analysis.[1]

The separation of church leadership concern for motivational push from the administrative focus on contextual pull enables a dimension to be highlighted that management theorists can do little with. This is where an individual's motives come from. In work organizations, these have to be recognized as a given that came in the door with the people who have them. For organizational participants already in place, managers are left to make the most out of what they have. In Christian fellowships, motives cannot be just a given. They are front and center as the very reason for being together. They are subject to the means by which God offers his life-changing grace. Pastors, even in their administrative role, dare not stray far from a profound respect for how the Holy Spirit pushes believers into action and the means by which he works.

In facing her volunteer problem, Pastor Proctor has two basic choices. She, with the committee, can conclude that the program context was arranged poorly and look for a way to rearrange the opportunities offered to the volunteers. I address this approach next as the delivery of satisfactions. Or she can conclude that they recruited the wrong volunteers, people whose action drives do not really match the program. This involves the stewardship of spiritual gifts, which is explored in the next section. Both factors are probably involved. Simply scolding the volunteers for lack of Christian commitment will likely reduce rather than increase their effort.

A Psychological Framework for Motivation

The key to administering the context for action by others is to offer them opportunities to satisfy a personal need they are ready to act on. Needs are the flip side of motives. A drive or desire does not emerge until an individual perceives that he or she is lacking something. Action springs from the desire to fill a need. To identify action opportunities that a person is likely to put energy into, one looks for the kind of need or needs that person is trying to fill at that time.

Psychologists have presented a variety of classifications to describe the needs that motivate human behavior. Many are oriented toward understanding abnormal or dysfunctional behavior, and these are the theories most familiar to pastors who have explored counseling psychology. Administrators spend most of their time working with relatively normal adults under relatively normal circumstances. The analytical framework of psychologist Abraham Maslow is especially helpful for understanding and predicting behavior under those circumstances.[2] It has become a basic reference point for the development of management insights on motivation. Pastoral administrators, too, can find it helpful, although we will have to be aware of some questions that arise in its application to the behavior of Christians in church life.

Maslow suggests that five basic needs motivate most human behavior. These are bodily needs, and the needs for security, for affiliation, for self-esteem, and for self-actualization.

He furthermore sees these needs appearing in a rough order or hierarchy of their power to stimulate action. The most basic are bodily needs. Until hunger and rest needs are satisfied, for instance, a person is not likely to devote much attention to other needs. Security, or the need for a predictable environment, is the next most basic. When security is threatened, the other, higher-level needs in the hierarchy lose much of their ability to focus energy on action. Affiliation and esteem can appear as motivators when the basic needs are fairly well satisfied. The need for self-actualization is difficult to define, but it describes the need a person feels to express what is distinctive and unique about him or herself. Self-actualization usually motivates behavior only when the other needs are well along the way to being met.

Maslow makes one other assumption that is important for managers to note. A satisfied need motivates little new behavior. The offer of a steak dinner, for instance, will have little appeal at the moment to someone who has just finished a full meal. That person will expend little energy to participate in a second meal.

In practical application, Maslow's approach can help explain what is going on when a person does not respond as a manager hopes. The intended action apparently does not satisfy a need that is important to the person at that time. This could be because, like a second meal, the hoped-for action would address a need already filled. Or it would satisfy a need that has not yet emerged as a motivator because the person is concentrating energy on more basic needs. In work organizations, the opportunity to address an esteem need through promotion to the supervisor rank will not elicit much new behavior from a person who feels a strong affiliation need to be accepted as a peer by current fellow workers.

With volunteer church workers, almost any of the needs highlighted by Maslow could lie behind their decision to offer their availability to do a task. Long-standing church members often approach church life as a means of satisfying security needs for familiar routines and a predictable future. With this need as a motivator, such volunteers may stay active in a program so long as it delivers the satisfaction of stable and familiar patterns of church activity. They can quickly lose interest in programs that involve them in significant changes.

The need to be close to others in supportive relationships of affiliation can be another strong motivator in church life. A dominant need to feel supported, however, does not necessarily turn into energy for initiating tasks, especially if such a volunteer is asked to make new relationships happen in an ambiguous situation. When affiliation needs are more readily satisfied in other relationships, a church program appealing to those needs will elicit a disappointing level of involvement from those who initially responded to that possibility. A satisfied need is no longer a motivator, and convenient satisfactions have a way of displacing inconvenient ones.

Esteem describes the need for recognition and respect from others. It can be a strong motivator in church life among people who are ready to place a high value on the opinions of others in the fellowship. Members frequently volunteer for tasks they think other respected members consider to be important. Should they conclude that the task, and therefore their involvement in it, is not so highly regarded, volunteers energized by esteem needs are likely to experience a significant loss of interest. The satisfaction to be delivered is respect and not necessarily something intrinsic in the task itself. Southard's discussion of power in a congregation especially addresses this need.

Self-actualization is sometimes described as the need for achievement, the need to express oneself in the accomplishment of something that an individual is uniquely capable of doing. Maslow suggests that this need is the least dominant motivator in human behavior. When present, it can produce exciting contributions to fellowship life that can enrich the lives of others and blaze new trails for them to follow. I see self-actualization, or achievement, as the motivating need at work among Christians who are acting out what the Spirit has gifted them to do in the body. More on this in the next section.

Application to the Case

The cluster program at Our Shepherd Church recruited fourteen volunteers, and the performance of most of them turned out to be disappointing. In all likelihood, the fourteen were acting on a variety of needs when they accepted this program responsibility. Most of the needs were apparently not satisfied. Indeed, the program seems poorly thought out and planned. Actually, the only satisfaction delivered seemed to go to the initiators. Pastor Proctor and the vocal committee members were probably acting on self-actualization needs to develop something unique in this congregation. And the need was probably rooted in their personal giftedness to take initiative in shepherding others. Their mistake was to project their own giftedness onto others.

How could the program be designed differently? For those motivated by a need to preserve the security of the familiar, the new fellowship effort would have to deliver the satisfaction of keeping existing groupings viable instead of starting what would appear to be competing groups. Security-oriented volunteers would need to see the new evolve out of the old for them to stay interested. In acting out their own needs, the fellowship planners probably did not communicate much regard for the old. If she is not careful, Pastor Proctor could find these members turning into active opponents of the program.

The group of cluster leaders almost certainly has some who volunteered out of esteem needs. If nothing else, they would value the respect of the pastor who stands behind the effort. But the program got started with minimal approval by other church leaders, and experience is showing that it is not considered important by most of the congregation. They have gotten little satisfaction and will get even less if the pastor and the committee communicate peevishness over their inactivity. The program would have to deliver success to address their needs. The planners can hardly get there from where they are now. If they want to try, they would have to almost start over again, concentrating on developing a more enthusiastic endorsement by other respected leaders and launching new clusters only after they have won recognition of the value of a first few. Southard shows how such endorsement can be won.

The volunteers who would seem most suited for the program would be those ready to act on a need for affiliation. This observation has implications for the selection process to be discussed later. Even if they had volunteered with this motivation, the committee still has a long way to go in developing a program context that delivers satisfaction to them. They have to find ways to reduce the difficulty of getting these leaders into meaningful relationships with their intended groups. Centralized scheduling of group gatherings might help. Specific requests from the pastor for help to care for specific families might facilitate the shepherding that is hoped for. As is, the cluster program seems highly unstructured (a common characteristic of the efforts of support-oriented leaders). Some volunteers find satisfaction in initiating structure, but they tend not to be the ones who are motivated by affiliation needs.

Training

Whatever their primary motivation, volunteers, like paid workers, have a hard time finding satisfaction trying to do a task they do not understand or they lack confidence to perform. The most direct administrative response is to offer training for the task. The purpose for such training is not just to get the job done reasonably well. It is also a basic way to increase the chances that the one doing the work will experience satisfaction.

Churches often seem particularly lax in carefully providing for the training of volunteer workers. This oversight may stem from poor definition of tasks to begin with, something that is a symptom of poor planning. Or it may mean that the work is not considered important enough to want it done well, an assumption that inevitably communicates a demotivating message to volunteers. Almost certainly, the oversight means that the church's leaders are not concentrating on the delivery of satisfaction to the members who agree to take on extra responsibilities. A church that does not make the effort to train workers is predictably a church where the pastor is going to complain about the problem of dealing with volunteers.

Satisfaction in a Theological Context

In these observations about how church leaders can but often fail administratively to move Christians into action, I have been applying an analytical framework commonly used in personnel management. The implicit point is that pastors themselves will find administration more rewarding if they become more skilled at personnel management.

The basics of personnel management seem sensible. Yet, they are so often neglected in churches. Part of the explanation may be that the image of a pastor has not included management responsibility for the work and welfare of others. But pastors may also carry a fundamental resistance to the starting assumption of the approach outlined here. As emphasized, the key to administering the context for action by others is to arrange for the delivery of satisfactions to them. Theologically, this emphasis may seem suspect.

Selfishness is another word for need gratification. To follow Christ includes heeding the call away from selfishness and toward selfless love of God and others. Christians should act according to God's will and the needs of their neighbors, not to satisfy their own needs. To preachers immersed in the theology of Christ-centered motivational push, the administrative concentration on the pull of a context for delivering self-oriented satisfaction can seem like unfaithful pandering to the sinful old nature Christians are to leave behind. To do so systematically would then be even worse than to make occasional concessions.

Theology and psychology remain in tension over this issue of need-based motivation. I will not pretend to offer a persuasive resolution to a very complicated question. But I will note that Christ enjoins us to love ourselves as much as our neighbors (Matt. 19:19; Mark 12:31). As God's creations, we Christians do remain human beings whose make-up is to act in ways that fill our needs as we perceive them. Fundamentally, the gospel can be seen as the good news of God's delivery of satisfaction for our basic needs for security, affiliation, esteem, and self-actualization. Church life can and should make concrete the delivery of such need satisfaction.

The central question of this chapter is how administrators move Christians into action. Even in a task orientation of seeing people as they can be, administrators can only respond to people as they are, not as they theoretically should be. Pastors are prone to define the needs of others according to their theological perspectives (e.g., "These people 'need' to study God's word more."). Administrators have to identify needs as they are perceived by the person to be "pulled" into action. Pastoral administrators who cannot make this conceptual adjustment will experience considerable frustration with their administrative role.

Administering the Application of Spiritual Gifts

Of course, the Holy Spirit is a factor in the motivational mix that goes into "stirring up one another to love and good works."

Under the Spirit's persuasion, our needs do change. The fruit of the Spirit affects the way we act on these needs—with love, joy, peace, patience, kindness, goodness, faithfulness, gentleness, and self-control (Gal. 5:22). These general workings of the Spirit refreshingly contribute to the personnel givens to which church administrators respond.

But there is a special working of the Spirit to which church leaders will want to be especially responsive. Our Lord promises that each member of the body will receive a manifestation of the Spirit for the common good (1 Cor. 12:7), and these spiritual gifts differ among the members. In other words, every participant in the fellowship can and will be moved by the Spirit to contribute something special beyond minimal participation in the routines of fellowship life. The lists of the gifts of the Spirit in Romans 12, 1 Corinthians 12, and Ephesians 4 are distinctly action and work oriented, in contrast to the character traits presented as the fruits of the Spirit. For leaders who look carefully, all members are differently pushed by the Spirit in this special way and are there to be recognized as the working parts of the fellowship.

In terms of motivational psychology, this manifestation of the Spirit creates something akin to a need for self-actualization within the fellowship. St. Paul urged: "Having gifts that differ according to the grace given to us, let us use them" (Rom. 12:6). Today, we could just as well say, "Satisfy your need to actualize the gift God has given uniquely to each of you."

This simple assumption about self-actualization of gifts transforms pastoral administration into personnel management in the fullest sense. The apostle Peter included such management in his charge to the faithful he was addressing in his First Epistle: "As each has received a gift, employ it for one another, as good stewards of God's varied grace" (4:10). His image of the steward fits right in with the image of a congregation as a house to be built. The Greek word *oikonomos* describes a person whose function it is to distribute goods and services (to oversee the economy) within a household. The English *steward* catches the household flavor of that term. But the more modern *manager* would be just as appropriate. Peter is not just urging that an individual be a good manager of his or her own gift. He writes in the plural. Together, we are to manage what we have been given by God's grace.

How can a diversity of gifted capabilities scattered among many individuals be managed? By getting them where they will do the

most good—by positioning them within the fellowship. Through
the Spirit's special motivation, a congregation has more than enough
people to get its work done. The leadership challenge is to get
specific potential contributions identified and then matched to
the right opportunity to do what each person is ready and willing to do.

In personnel management, this leadership function amounts to
recruitment and selection. Without careful management, finding
workers is often done haphazardly. As experienced church members
can attest, churches have a way of simply calling on the members
who conveniently come to mind when there is a job at hand. All
sorts of odd and frustrating matches get made this way, as Pastor
Proctor and the fellowship committee discovered.

It is common-sense management first to develop extensive knowledge of the available membership capabilities and of the known
places where there is work to be done. Then a match between
the gifted person and the needed task can be deliberately and
carefully made. The result is much greater assurance of arriving
at the best match for the individual and for those who are served.

Such selection depends on thorough identification of the gifts
present in the fellowship. The most direct way to do that is to
ask each member what he or she likes to do, has a history of
doing, does well, and is willing to do in the congregation. There
is more to gift identification than that, but it is a good start. Most
congregational leaders have such knowledge about some members
informally. Why not do that for all members formally? This is
what a personnel manager would aim for. He or she will often
develop information on each person from forms and questionnaires
to extend knowledge beyond limited firsthand observation.

What would happen if each member of a congregation were
asked to fill out a questionnaire designed to highlight his or her
particular gifts? It is possible to find out. Such a questionnaire
has been developed and extensively used by the Fuller Institute
of Evangelism and Church Growth.[3]

What will probably happen, according to church leaders who
systematically use this gift-identification approach, is that not only
selection but also recruitment is done more effectively. While discovering gifts is important for the congregation, it is even more
important for the individual believer. Most are not used to thinking
about themselves as possessors of something special and God-given
to contribute. Even St. Paul had to remind the people in his

churches. When modern-day believers discover this for themselves, their readiness to invest time and energy in sharing their gifts is heightened. This is not just a theory. It actually happens. A "gift's discovery" questionnaire is received by many as a call to work.

The experience of a Detroit-area church, St. Paul's Lutheran, is available as a case example. Their story is reported in *Leadership*. [4] The outwardly visible results are encouraging (a tripling of Sunday morning attendance in seven years and an even greater increase in financial offerings). But more important is a high degree of enthusiasm reported among members who are discovering specifically what they can do, where they are needed, and how meaningful church work can be. In the words of one trustee craftsman, "When you are gifted to do something, and you, the pastors, and the congregation know it, then a phone call for your services just seems natural." From the viewpoint of the pastor, "Our people feel they have ownership here."

This church's full-time minister of spiritual gifts operates with two basic tools: an eighty-five item spiritual gifts analysis form, which all members are expected to fill out, and a development and use form, which lists more than two hundred places to serve. After taking the spiritual gifts analysis, a member checks each area he or she wants to be involved in. The gifts administrator then catalogs the responses and contacts the administrator of each board, committee, or gifts area who can use those gifts. He leaves it to each administrator to contact the person and put him or her to work. Fundamental to the effectiveness of this program is this congregation's very clear expectation that each member will help out in some way beyond normal attendance.

In terms of the building function of pastoral administration, this kind of management is contractor ministry done thoroughly and skillfully. It is done in the context of church life that has benefited from an architectural ministry focused on designing outcomes and relationships.

This kind of administration also amounts to something more than leading volunteers. Pastors have been too willing to buy into the volunteer model and vocabulary for thinking about unpaid workers. Churches potentially have a different motivational base than the Red Cross or the local hospital has to deal with. Unpaid workers in the church need to be treated at least as well as hospital volunteers. But regarding a Spirit-gifted worker as only a volunteer detracts from the expectation that all in the fellowship are inspired by God to minister to the common good.

Fitting Workers and Tasks Together

When presented with the possibilities that flow from congregational recognition of the gifts of the Spirit, pastors often turn skeptical. They see an approach that is very different from what they have grown accustomed to. It is just this difference, though, that becomes one of the keys to finding pastoral joy in administration. One reaction is that it just won't work. A picture of everyone ready to step forward as church workers does not square very well with the common pastoral experience of the difficulty of moving members into action. To be sure, simply adopting a new "gifts" program for next year is no guarantee that all other programs will suddenly take off. A change in the vitality of a congregation depends on the seriousness and thoroughness with which the spiritual base for life together is pursued. A new way to "pull" members into action can bring some improvement but not nearly as much as comes with a new recognition of the "push" that precedes action. Whether or not a pastor believes Christians will really act as God-gifted workers depends on his or her belief in the power of the Holy Spirit. St. Paul certainly believed. This conviction formed the basis of his whole ministry.

Another reaction is that, if it did work, pastors would not know what to do with the results. They would have many more workers than they could possibly know how to use. Veteran pastors fear one more administrative failure. Indeed, arranging the contextual pulls for the hundreds of activated Christians necessitates good administration. Then the stewardship responsibility cannot be avoided. But present among all those motivated workers are undoubtedly a number of gifted administrators. They can share in finding solutions to this "problem" of too much energy. Pastors need fear only if they still operate with the image of carrying the leadership function alone.

At issue is whether church leaders will try to fit members into assigned tasks or try to fit tasks around interested individuals. The first approach is the customary way. It brings known frustrations to all involved. The latter approach taps much more energy and opens up new possibilities for building fellowship life.

Actually there is a middle ground. Programs can be launched before all the needed workers are excited about the effort—if there is a means to identify members who could, on their own terms, find satisfaction through such involvement.

Pastor Proctor and the fellowship committee were way ahead of the people of Our Shepherd Church. This could be good leadership for the shared journey of this fellowship. The administrative mistake was insufficient attention to the selection and training of the workers. Their program needed cluster leaders with the gift of shepherding, or pastoring. In God's providence, 5 to 10 percent of the members could well be so gifted, at least in seminal form. When stewards of God's gifts take the time to find and nurture them, these potential workers would be pulled into action—with enthusiasm for all involved.

SOUTHARD

Empowering Church Programs

Pastor Proctor and her people have not been able to keep their promises to each other. They believe that a shepherding program to all the members is essential to the Christian fellowship, but there is no sustaining power for the program.

How can the pastor and the people help each other to keep their promises? In this particular case, the problem seems to be implementation. Good decisions have been made, some of the right people are involved, and the intentions move toward godly goals, but there is no enduring strength. There is no day-to-day infusion of power into proposals that seem so promising.

The empowering of any activity of the Christian fellowship is based on the promise of the risen Lord: "You shall receive power when the Holy Spirit has come upon you; and you shall be my witnesses" (Acts 1:8). Paul applies this promise to the building up of a congregation through policies and structures when he concludes a discussion of gifts of the Spirit with the statement, "For God is not a God of confusion but of peace" (1 Cor. 14:33).

The Spirit not only guides us into channels for the expression of love but also provides the means by which the aim of divine love is transformed into human action. The ideal is a demonstration of Spirit and power together (1 Cor. 2:4).

When the Spirit is manifest in power, good intentions and personal commitment can be translated into specific enduring programs through the church. This combination of Spirit and power has been portrayed in Christian art and sculpture as a dove hovering over a council of church leaders, a group of magistrates, or an assembly of learned persons. Wisdom and good counsel were the particular blessings that came to powerful persons who made decisions.[5]

How do we practice these gifts of the Spirit to put power into what we are administering? The answer is to be found in our faithful pursuit of basic questions in relationships between individuals and the larger organization of which they are a part. These questions require a pastoral interest, an alert observation of how people relate to each other, an intuitive understanding of the way they receive and react to responsibilities in the congregation, patience and courage in moving through the multitude of misunderstandings, waywardness of attention, and special pleading and general discouragement that creep into all encounters of Christians with one another. The implementation of programs is like a constant winnowing of wheat from chaff, a continual movement in which we hope that the good we do will survive and the imperfect will pass away.

Four questions will assist us in this process of continuing power:

- How is power distributed in the congregation?
- What issues will receive attention?
- How can we support those who show an interest?
- Can power flow through a variety of leadership styles?

These questions reflect how I look at administration differently than Luecke. I see routine functions in more relational terms. He concentrates on arranging a context that will pull activities from participants. I would concentrate on relationships that recognize and sustain power. It is significant that I choose to focus on power. This in itself is a relational concept. It describes the ability of one person to influence another.

The differences become more apparent if we consider a frequently used classification of the bases of social power. Social psychologists French and Raven outline five possible bases from which a person or group can exercise power: (1) the ability to coerce, (2) the ability to reward, (3) having the legitimate right, (4) being respected as a person, and (5) having valued expertise.[6]

Neither Luecke nor I advocate coercive power, although pastors often rely on it through efforts to induce feelings of guilt. Luecke prefers to work with reward power, as evidenced in his theme of delivering satisfactions. I prefer to work with personal power, not necessarily my own but that of others in the church, and also the expert power of giving others guidance. Legitimate power given to a leader by the people is something that has to be earned by a pastor. Either of our approaches can increase such legitimacy.[7]

Where Is the Power?

In a study of the people who made up the leadership in Dallas, Texas, a sociologist asked two hundred of them for names of people they would turn to when they needed advice or approval to get something done in the city. One of the people whose name appeared very frequently was asked why he was chosen. He replied that he associated with people who had the power to assign subordinates a community task and not worry about their time off from the job. He also thought that he was associated with people who put the good of the city ahead of their personal ambitions. They were respected for who they were and for what they could command.

When we ask this kind of question in the local church and look for the characteristics that have just been described, we will know where the power resides. Sometimes, we will find that those who are respected for putting the good of the church ahead of their own personal ambitions will be members of official boards. Sometimes, they will not be visible in that particular way. But people who have been in the community for some period of time will know whom they can respect and trust for decisions and turn to them.

Whether we discover power among those who are official leaders or those who are natural leaders, we would know that these people have the most influence in the congregation.

Of course, we are not sure at the time, or at any time, as to the extent of spiritual power in these influential people. One part of the winnowing process is to work long enough with powerful people to see the dominance of the Spirit over all other forces that give a person credibility in a congregation. What we do know is the importance of these people in any enduring program in the church.

Better recognition of this important factor in the keeping of promises does not mean a complete subservience to key leaders. Instead, our identification of those with power is only one part of our answer to the question, For what purpose is power needed? When we look at power from this operational perspective, we free spiritual force to work both in those who are identified as powerful persons and in those who have more limited strength in the eyes of others.

The identification of powerful people is only a precondition of another part of promise keeping, which is the distribution of power in various activities and emphases of the church. This will answer the question, Where is the power?—both in individuals and in programs.

When we relate people and programs, we are then ready for an operational question: What kind of power is most appropriate for a particular program? We must know the place of a program in the life of the church and the way it is supposed to function. Then we can seek people with gifts and grace necessary for the task. This is leadership—the powerful combination of person and position for agreed-upon purposes.

What are some of the typical combinations of power that are needed in a congregation?

1. When there is general agreement about a major ongoing function of the congregation, a person with high visibility as a church and community leader will provide power to implement the program.

A major fund-raising drive would be an occasion to find someone with this status. Churches who obtain such leadership will have less difficulty in soliciting support than those who rely on newcomers and complex procedures to build commitment. In one study of church management, "St. James" Episcopal Church violated social norms by using a new resident as the fulcrum for stewardship education. Consultants for the program found that the education sessions, held in homes, were well attended in the homes of well-established families of status and poorly attended in the homes of newer members.[8]

2. A newcomer with spiritual interests and program experience in a needed area of church growth may soon become a center of influence when an untried program is presented. This will be effective if established leaders are not opposed to this development. The pastor's recommendations and interests are often decisive in the early stages of these programs.

3. When a shift of emphasis is imminent, transition is less traumatic when there are some old and new leaders in favor of a new movement. This provides a distribution of power that calls for some majority judgment. If the pastor will consult both the old and new leaders, he will probably establish new coalitions of interest that will move the church with strength through a time of change.

4. When various people agree that an objective is desirable but disagree on the ways to achieve it, power must be modulated. That is, the objective must not be promoted or pushed by one powerful person who may not be aware of what others think about his or her pet project. Some compromises must be worked out so that people can contribute various degrees of power from various points of view to obtain a solution. The solution may not be as satisfactory to one or two powerful people as it may be to many of less power who can live with compromise.

5. When there is no agreement on consequences, and the church seems to be on "dead center," a charismatic leader can mobilize power toward one objective. Most often this is the pastor and this is the style of leadership often praised in the literature when "old First Church" suddenly comes to life.

Power may stay over a period of time with one person because of general community influence, but the power for the ongoing purposes of the church will never stay in one place. Some people have high potential for general leadership, while others are most essential in the performing of specific tasks. Some subjects gather immediate interest and require the kind of strength that comes from leaders with great enthusiasm, while other tasks require much staff work, negotiations, and long periods of building. The pastor will need to know the communication network of the congregation if he or she is going to find the right combination between spiritual power and personal influence.

What Are the Issues?

The power of leadership is never completely confined to the characteristics of a leader. The issues at hand and the configuration of the congregation will also be significant. For this reason, we must talk about the actual issues in implementing a program along with the characteristics and visibility of the leaders for such programs.

One way to combine these questions is to think in every organizational meeting about this question: Power for what? There are several ways in which this question comes to us.

Who raised the issue and why? The answer to this question came to me differently in two pastorates. In one pastorate, I found that Sunday school officers and teachers were visiting prospects. I sought to use this interest as an opportunity to develop a shepherding program for all members of the congregation. But I soon found that the primary interest of these leaders was in Christian education rather than in pastoral care. After several months, I saw that my efforts were unsuccessful.

In another pastorate, three men with high visibility as church and community leaders were very interested in a type of pastoral care program that had been developed by Elton Trueblood. They asked if I would support a yoke-fellow program if I became pastor; I told them that I certainly would. The program was worked out between the four of us. Within a month after I became pastor, the program was accepted by the congregation and, within six months, we had trained deacons for pastoral care responsibilities and visitation of all church members and prospects.

Obviously, in the first pastorate, I had raised the issue of pastoral care and my power was very limited. In the second pastorate, three influential persons had raised the issue and when I cooperated with them, the program was effective.

We may find that some emphases of the church have been developed over a very long period of time by some influential person. Grace Goodwin found that "again and again, church members pointed to a particular adult-class leader, or a planning committee, or a prophetic former pastor who dug up the ground and planted the seeds of new ideas that later leaders could bring to harvest." [9]

When does this proposal become church business? Many initial proposals for the church are not implemented because they are illegitimate. That is, they have no family background acceptable to those who set standards and make decisions for the community. A program that goes through the process of legitimization, however, will enjoy acceptance and some success.

One of the most powerful agencies for adoption of ideas during the twentieth century has been the denomination. As Dr. Tom

Bennett found in the Effective City Church study, the laity sees the denomination as an organization of power and prestige, represented in the community by the pastor.[10] A denominational program will usually be a source of power in mobile, urban areas where there is no existing community structure, friendship pattern, or common mores. The denomination provides something familiar to many people, or at least it is a common source of identification.

In more settled areas of the country, denominational endorsement may be of little consequence. People know who they can trust for decisions about the church and are very informal about program procedures. Donald Zimmerman and Arleon Kelley found that the further a church was from Indianapolis, the state headquarters for a certain denomination, the less acceptance there was of denominational proposals. Twenty-five miles seemed to be the effective range of immediate acceptance of any new idea from Indianapolis into the countryside.[11]

Who is consistently interested? The inauguration of an activity depends upon the interests and talents of volunteers. Except for the case of the charismatic leader, a program does not survive without the continuing motivation of a core of interested people. The pastor's task is to assist leaders in the selection of people who are both committed to a program and confident to implement it. Then conditions must be created under which these people are supported by the congregation's policies and procedures in carrying out the promises to which they are pledged.

What are the conditions under which motivation will be consistent and leaders will have increasing satisfaction through their organizational responsibility? The question can be answered in terms of a difference between "motivators" and "dissatisfiers."

"Motivators" are the factors of achievement, responsibility, growth, advancement, work itself, and earned recognition. Frederick Hertzberg and others found these to be the essential ingredients in the studies that they conducted of satisfied employees. "Dissatisfiers" came through problems with the policy of the company, inadequate supervision, poor working conditions, and marginal salary.[12]

As volunteers serve the church, their highest motivator is "a feeling of serving God through his church."[13] This is sustained through recognition of achievement and a sense of mutual responsibility with the professional staff for the growth and advancement of the church.

How does a pastor contribute to this sense of adequate service among volunteers? The essential issue is the pastor's attitude for those who are associated in kingdom service and the procedures by which people see on a regular basis that they are honored in what they do. As John Henry Felix, a member of the International Board of the Red Cross, has found in a generation of work with volunteers, volunteer motivation is high when they are treated exactly like professionals on the paid staff of an organization.[14]

How Can the Pastor Provide Support?

Most of what I have just written about the identification of power has already been done in the development of the shepherding program by Pastor Proctor and the fellowship committee. People who had specific interest in pastoral care were probably on the fellowship committee and those who were recruited to lead a cluster fellowship did meet their promises for at least one year. But there seemed to be some gap between the continuing motivation of the original numbers of the fellowship committee and the other cluster leaders who joined with them in pastoral care. This is one sign of trouble, in relation to the question of identified power. Has the program expanded beyond those who were motivated to continue it?

There also may be some problems in the procedures that were followed by the pastor with the shepherding program. The brief review of the case does not tell us much about this, but I would suspect that there are problems of procedures here, as often there are in the reports of doctor of ministry projects by pastors who have organized a shepherding program. In the field reports of pastors in fifteen programs that I supervised between 1980 and 1985, two major difficulties were observable. The first is a lack of training for the volunteers who serve as associates with the pastor in the care of members. The other problem is a lack of support for the group of care-givers. Essentially, both problems revolve around the issue of support systems provided either by the pastor or the pastor in association with serving leaders of the congregation.

This may well be one of the problems for the cluster volunteers who disappointed Pastor Proctor. Some have responded with enthusiasm to their responsibilities, but neither the pastor nor the fellowship committee report any efforts to train or sustain them in a continuing ministry.

How do we provide the kind of support that will move people consistently toward program objectives that are consistent with their Christian commitment? In a study of effective pastors, James Ashbrook found five items that combined skillful and inspiring leadership. They were:

- the ability to define roles,
- to structure expectations,
- to take initiative,
- to accept some leadership ambiguity and uncertainty, and
- to encourage freedom among members who accept leadership.[15]

Defining roles. Were the cluster volunteers in Pastor Proctor's congregation to do the work of a pastor and to be respected in the role? We do not know from the case study. But we can well imagine the uncertainty of volunteers who are confronted by some serious personal difficulty in their cluster or who are asked some ecclesiastical question by a disgruntled member. Should the volunteer accept responsibility for the problem or make a referral to the pastor?

The first question to be settled would be the expectation of the congregation and the pastor concerning these volunteers. Clarity can be achieved when the pastor presents the meaning of the congregational care program in a sermon, a church letter, or a special meeting of the congregation. I found that it was helpful not only to give these explanations but also to visit with the volunteer caregivers when I was a pastor. With each family, we would explain that this volunteer would serve as a pastor to the people in this cluster. I as the senior pastor would serve as a player coach, one who was available whenever necessary but always as one member of a team in which all of us combined the function and status of the pastoral office. I do not think it is necessary for every pastor to agree with my definition of the relationship between ordained and unordained persons in the performance of ministry. But I do think it is essential for the role of the layperson to be clearly defined before the care-giving program can begin with any continuing source of strength.

Structuring expectations. We do know from the case study that each volunteer was responsible for fifteen or twenty adults in a given geographical area and that there were to be several meetings a year for Bible study and fellowship. Some additional expectations might need to be clarified as a program develops; but at least, the volunteers know how much they can do within a given period of time. So long as the administrative requirements are not excessive, our volunteers can feel that they are making a contribution that will be respected by the pastor and the congregation. Their motivation will not be reduced by a sense of guilt in not doing all that they thought they had promised to do.

From a pastor's perspective, it is essential that the senior minister should be in weekly or monthly contact with most of the volunteers as they go through the first year of this kind of ministry. Expectations often have to be changed in the light of the changing circumstances of the volunteers and some of the problems that they meet in their ministry. For example, I found in one of my pastorates that two of the cluster leaders were very discouraged because most of the members assigned to them were "dormant" church members. Dormant members had no real interest in the life of the congregation and did not wish to participate. Other cluster leaders felt enthusiastic because their visits were to "intermittent" church members, people who still cared for the church but were careless in their Christian commitment. Visits to these people produced appreciation from those who were visited and usually an increase in their church attendance.

When we became aware of this difficulty, some reassignment of people in the cluster was made so that one or two volunteers were not continually disappointed with the visits to dormant members.

Taking initiative. If the pastor is defined as a player coach and the volunteers as associate pastors, then some expectation of initiative is shared by all members of the team. But at the same time, the pastor as coach must show a general concern for all of the cluster volunteers. This may begin with work in the fellowship committee to choose the people who are to be the cluster volunteers. It would also be necessary for the pastor to preach or teach about this program from time to time and to make it clear that the professional staff gives full support to this important fellowship contribution.

Then there is the question of watchfulness in relation to motivation. Do some of the volunteers drop out of a training program before it is completed? Why? Do others provide no reports of meetings with members of their cluster? Is there some problem of motivation or of structure? Are there complaints from members of the congregation concerning the meetings that they have with the cluster volunteers? Are there complaints from cluster volunteers themselves? In all of these instances, the pastor must take initiative to provide supervision, support, and clarification.

One way to institutionalize this initiative would be a schedule through which the pastor went with one or two volunteers on their first meetings with members of the cluster. These cooperative visitations could continue every few months, so that each volunteer has the pastor's personal support of the pastor on a regular basis.

It was during these regular visits with the volunteers that I became aware of some of the problems that cause people to drop away from care-giving programs. Problems were reported that seemed unsolvable to the volunteers. There were expressions of concern about the way that some people were receiving a visit, or there was a sense of unworthiness and uncertainty in the volunteers' conversations. I encouraged the volunteers to bring these reports to the monthly meeting of care-givers in order that all of us might share in these kinds of problems and see how we could learn from them to be more effective in our ministry in the future.

In contrast, my visits to some churches in which there are "yoke-fellow" ministries has identified a drop in enthusiasm when some "problem" case occurred, and the pastor knew nothing about the difficulty. As more and more problem cases emerged on a spasmodic basis throughout the congregation, volunteers decreased their contacts with members of their cluster community. There was a general fear that work was not being done well. People withdrew from that which foreboded failure.

Accepting ambiguity and uncertainty. Some of the fifteen pastors who developed a cluster care program might have rejected the development of a support system because they did not wish to deal with questions of hesitation and uncertainty in the membership. They would have preferred to launch the program with lay leadership and then move on to some other development.

But there is no program in a church that does not require continuing pastoral support, especially a program in which life's uncertainties and the members' hopes and fears are shared with one another. If people are to keep their promises to one another in a pastoral care program, they must recognize that these promises are being given as a limited human being to other human beings. We are not able to foresee and plan for all the difficulties that may arise in the development of a program or provide the type of training that will give immediate answers to every difficulty that is expressed by a member during a pastoral visit.

Once we recognize the inevitable uncertainty and ambiguity of any program that brings people in contact with each other for higher purposes, we could recognize the importance of the faith and hope that Paul combined with love in his writing about a basic Christian commitment (1 Cor. 13). Those who use the gifts that God has provided for them must do so with an awareness of the everyday need for patience, humility, courage, and perseverance.

If we plan with this "sober judgment," then we are more aware of the Spirit's power in all that we perform. There is a recognition of problems that are insoluble from a human point of view, obstacles that appear beyond the limits of our human vision. A humble recognition of that which we cannot control by human means is the opportunity for the heart to be open before the steadfast love that empowers people who embrace the Spirit's leadership.

Is It Done My Way?

Is it possible for a pastor to clarify goals, structure expectations, take initiative, and still tolerate hesitancy and uncertainty? To do so would not only be an exercise in humility and faith, but it would also be a recognition that each cluster leader would bring a particular style to the care-giving activity and each member would have varying expectations of the care that would be received. Unless this wide variation in expectations is met through some common motivation, programs cannot proceed with power.

When we consider the diversity of gifts and the unexpected problems of administration, we must ask a very searching question of ourselves as leaders: Do we want the power to be concentrated according to our style of doing things? Admittedly, the answer is yes if we have a strong charismatic style that is needed in a church that is moribund and uncertain. But this is a very specialized use of power in a particular situation. Our concern is to recognize a variety of leadership styles that are appropriate both in the pastor and in the people for particular situations or at the time when each problem or program is of unique importance.

Can power flow through a variety of leadership styles? Two hundred graduate business students were quizzed with this question in mind. Professors McKenney and Keen found two general types of problem solving among these future business leaders: systematic thinkers, who plan and organize, and intuitive thinkers, who excel if a problem is elusive and difficult to define.

Billy Graham was given by the researchers as an example of systematic thinking. He knows what he believes and what is the ultimate solution. So, when listening to someone in trouble, he can size up the predicament rapidly and offer counsel.

Intuitive thinkers, however, receive more than they perceive. They focus on details, digest and ponder individual facts. They get a feel for the information and suspend judgment until they have tried out several solutions.

Does more power flow through one of these ways of thinking than the other? No. In tests of problem solving, McKenney and Keen found that neither type of thinking is superior. The successful manager is one who works at tasks suited to his or her problem-solving abilities at the right time.[16]

With eagerness to keep promises and to get the job done, some pastors may feel justified in insisting on their own way. But with the variety of functions to be performed in one congregation and the changes in circumstances that develop with each program, we need the continual reminder of the apostle Paul that we work for the common good with diverse gifts. A leader may channel power through the initiation of structure, the explanation of expectations, and the continual support of those who mobilize resources with him. But the leader cannot maximize spiritual power in this process unless there is an admission of limitations and gratitude for other styles of leadership. Then each person can be empowered in the contribution of unique gifts for the common good.

Summary

We both recognize how, as administrators, pastors are especially exposed to the problem of how to get people to do things. They are constantly developing programs that depend for their success on the movement of others. These others have to keep their promises in order for a pastoral administrator to keep his or her administrative promises.

Southard looks on this inherent plight of administrators in relational terms. He urges pastors to concentrate on the flow of power in the network of relations between church members. Recognizing which people have how much power is basic, as is identifying the issues to which they are likely to apply their power.

Luecke looks on the administrator's task as a matter of arranging the context within which individuals will want to move themselves. Motivation is his key concept, comparable to power for Southard. Administrators cannot "push" into action, they can only "pull" by providing opportunities for action that will deliver satisfaction to the motivation had by others.

In power terms, we emphasize different bases of power from which administrators can work. Luecke prefers reward power. Southard prefers expert power and the personal power some seem naturally to have. Neither of us recommends coercive power, like laying on guilt. We both see the right to expect compliance as a legitimate power a pastor has to earn through the judicious use of the other power bases.

We both see the Holy Spirit as the fundamental base of motivation and power in church life. Southard moves right from the Lord's promise that his people will receive the power of the Holy Spirit (Acts 1:8) to looking for evidence of the Spirit's power in the movements that can be seen among the Christians gathered as a congregation. Luecke looks to the Lord's promise that each member of the body will receive a manifestation of the Spirit for the common good (1 Cor. 12:7). He tries to fit these individual spiritual gifts, a form of self-actualizing motivation, to the church tasks where they will do the most good.

6

How Administrators Can Deal with Conflict

The Associate Pastor

Pastor Reese survived heart surgery several months ago, but he wasn't so sure that he would survive an emerging administrative conflict. He sounded very unsure of himself and the situation as he talked with a seminary classmate of twenty years ago, who was now his district superintendent:

PASTOR: Look, George, this is not like that problem I had with the educational director three years ago. She was too pushy in putting through our new curriculum. She made some members of the finance committee furious. They weren't going to be "graded by age" when they studied the Bible! So when there were complaints, I waited until she had the new program in place, then I let her go. Educational staff are expendable, you know.

But this is different. Zeke is ordained. He's an associate pastor. I can't just fire him like I could that girl. And besides, Joyce and Mabel have taken every course he's offered on liturgy, and their husbands are on the finance committee. I can't afford to have any trouble there.

GEORGE: Why not?

PASTOR: Because—you know—we never subscribe our budget! We're always short and owe money every summer. Then the men on the finance committee decide in November that they can give more to save on income tax, and we meet all our bills by Christmas! So I don't want to get on their bad side. And worst of all, Zeke goes to their homes for dinner, and they quote what he says about the new liturgy. What am I to do?

GEORGE: Well, why do you have to do anything, if Zeke is doing a good job?

PASTOR: He's becoming the expert on liturgy, and that *isn't* his job. I'm the senior pastor and worship leader. He's taken over too much. He confers with the music director about the order of worship and the hymns and the anthems. And Joyce and Mabel know that he knows more than I, ah, he talks like he knows more. I sat down and told him that I was writing manuals on worship before he was born. And he just smiled at me.

GEORGE: He's taken over the worship from you?

PASTOR: Well, not exactly a takeover. He's developed this interest and borrows my books; and I did ask him a year or so ago to plan the worship service. (Pause.) You see, I just don't have time for all that staff stuff. When I come to the office, I have people to see who need my counsel. So I stopped the weekly staff meetings. Zeke and the music director plan the service, I give them a sermon topic, and then I don't have to listen to all their tug-of-war with the new educational director.

GEORGE: So you let them run the church by, ah, default, shall we say?

PASTOR: You know how busy I am! I put in a full day, but it's getting away from me. Zeke asked for a huge raise. I told him we had to give more to missions and were behind on contributions. But Joyce and Mabel talked their husbands into it, and that raise was in the budget proposal by the finance committee before I knew it! And it passed.

GEORGE: So you're getting annoyed.

PASTOR: And now he has a youth retreat planned to study worship during the week that we emphasize world missions. The youth will be away when we have our great thrust for mission commitment. And did he tell me about it? No. I just saw it in the church calendar.

GEORGE: He plans the calendar?

PASTOR: Ah, the staff does that. And then he wanted one of his former professors to be the world missions speaker and talked it over with the missions chairperson. She supported him even when I said that we didn't have the money for that kind of speaker—we needed to use a retired missionary who lives near here.

GEORGE: Again, he was in control, and you hadn't checked with the chairperson?

PASTOR: No. I thought we'd do like we always do. I'd suggest someone when I got around to it. They always took my recommendations in the past.

But now it's different. They don't want my kind of missions speaker. They want someone from Zeke's seminary. He's all mystical and social action and no evangelism. It makes me sick to see where our church is drifting—and the money's behind it!

Look, should I do something about this or just wait for a reappointment or something?

SOUTHARD

Respecting Resistance

It seems strange to call Reese a "pastor" because he seems to have no support instinct. That is, when he senses trouble, there is no swift and sure search for suggestions and actions that will help conflicting people cope with changes in the common life of Christ. Maybe he does some of this in his individual counsel, but there seems to be no tie-in of relational conflict with participation in the church organization. In fact, he avoids organization because he considers it to be the place where conflicts are continuing to disturb him.

Is there any way that Pastor Reese could become a pastoral administrator, a person who serves with others in a covenant community where difficulties may emerge despite commitment and where common goals are related to individual needs?

The answer can be positive if Pastor Reese can view some conflict as an alarm bell of threatened personal values. On many occasions, the resistance of a person or a group is a way to determine that which is most significant to those people. If we find that their values are worth fighting for, then we can respect their resistance. If they in turn esteem our goals, then mutual respect can become a basis for the resolution of conflict. This is highly possible in a Christian fellowship where specific values are central, such as love, faith, hope, confession, forgiveness, and reconciliation. We might add, for Pastor Reese's motivation, that the resolution of marital conflict often depends upon renewed commitment to common values and also there must be respect for objectives in life that are unique in each spouse. If Pastor Reese receives training as a counselor, he'll learn the same principles of conflict resolution that apply in administration.

I should qualify all this with the word *sometimes,* because the values with which we identify may be either constructive or destructive. For example, if Pastor Reese finds that worship is the basic value that appeals to Zeke and evangelism is the basic value that appeals to Pastor Reese, then a constructive settlement is possible because of the godly nature of the values that need to be brought in harmony with one another. But if Pastor Reese finds that his own motivation is a senile search for status in a changing church, the conflict may be destructive. It will be even more devastating if his associate is also primarily dedicated to power and is using a virtue such as worship to extend personal interest.

How are we to know if the resistance is redemptive or irremediable? The first answer is in Pastor Reese himself.

Learning When You're Losing

I think that the district superintendent is coming to the same conclusion with Pastor Reese to which most of us would come. A middle-aged administrator is losing his position to a younger associate, partly by default and partly by a change of basic goals in the congregation. If Pastor Reese is going to find anything redemptive in this conflict, he must first redeem himself.

A redemptive perspective of conflict begins with the self because the relationship of all virtues is governed by prudence. That is, no decision about a value, no correlation of one virtue with another is productive unless it begins in a realistic evaluation of self and others. This is the basic meaning of prudence, the ability to know who we are and how we feel in a particular situation, along with some understanding of the feelings and responses of others.

How would prudence apply to Pastor Reese? The district superintendent could begin this process by asking his old friend: "What is the worst thing that could happen to you in this situation?" If the conversation is insightful, the pastor would probably conclude that he does not want to look foolish, to appear defensive, or to appear anxious about security and status. These would be helpful thoughts, for they involve Pastor Reese as a person in the conflict. If the superintendent is psychologically alert, he can show the connection between Pastor Reese's personal fears and the perceived administrative threats to his security. Is the pastor willing to look more prudently at himself? If so, then he will have taken a giant step toward the resolution of conflict in a redemptive direction. Even if he objects that the conflict is irremediable, the superintendent can help him to see that he has done something redemptive for himself by an honest analysis of himself in conflict.

Let us suppose that Pastor Reese is willing to be prudent. He can then connect self-perception with the question: "What is the worst that can happen to me?" Then he will be on his way to the central issue in most conflicts, which is dissonant values. He will have an opportunity to review the virtues that are most important to him as a Christian and as a pastor. The worst that could happen to him would be the loss of one of these values. This recognition of value will not only provide a perspective from which he can look more objectively upon the situation, it will also lead him to ask the same question about other people who are in conflict with him. What values are most important to them?

Will this kind of analysis really make a difference if we are in a losing situation? By this, I mean circumstances that inexorably move us toward the loss of position, status, salary, friendship, or valued service? When I went through such an experience, I wrote out some of the values that I would keep even when I knew that I would be losing a good deal. These are some of my statements:

- Use the situation to learn the humility that has always eluded you.
- Observe the impact of another person's power, rage, anxiety, and duplicity upon your own life and ask in what way are you the same.
- Seek the counsel of others to find out how much of this is in you.
- Listen to criticisms from another person who is hostile to you, without necessarily agreeing with the adversary, for this is a chance to hear what the person really thinks of you and how that person really thinks deep in himself.
- Learn limitations. Accept the ability of a powerful person to hurt you in some way.

- Do not lose too much by being anxious about the loss you cannot control.
- Concentrate on seeing yourself and refrain from a diagnosis of a contender, which is usually distorted when you are under stress.
- Whatever you see in another person, see it with mercy.
- Meditate upon how vulnerable and miserable you would be if you raged in the same way.

About a year after I composed these notes in a time of conflict, I met a former colleague who commented on the outcome. "You're the only person that [the adversary] was not able to draw blood from. You didn't go away wounded. You seem to have learned something even when you were losing something."

The Limits of Constructive Conflict

We not only learn by asking: "What is the worst that could happen to me?" We also learn by asking: "What is the best that can redeem this situation?"

Both of these questions must be asked. The first is asked so that we may see the reasons for our own resistance, clarify our values, cleanse ourselves of misconceptions and resentments, and diminish defensiveness. When this is being accomplished, we are making room for recognition of redemptive elements in the conflict situation. We are preparing ourselves internally to receive others' feelings about a situation in which we are mutually entangled. Our perception of the issues has improved, our readiness to be a vulnerable human being with others is more appealing.

A prudent person is aware of resources and obstacles in others as well as in himself. Such a person will also recognize the way in which people are related to each other and the importance of community tradition, circumstances that impinge upon the present problem, modes of communication in the organization and the community that make a difference in perception and communication. The prudent person hears himself and is then ready to hear others.

When we turn from self-readiness to an awareness of others, we recognize the interdependence that is an important part of conflict resolution. We do not blame ourselves completely for what has happened, and we do not blame any other person for all that has transpired. We try to understand our mutual dependence in the body of Christ. This attitude will reduce our own defensiveness against others because we will not feel completely guilty. Instead, we will be curious to know how the values that are important to us and the values that are important to others have been misperceived or misaligned. This approach will not only reduce our own sense of unworthiness, it will also assure others that we consider them to be worthy. Our first concern is not to place blame either upon others or upon ourselves.

Mutual dependence is sustained in the body of Christ when specific values are present in individual leaders and in their relationships with one another. At least four of these are of special importance for a redemptive approach to conflict:

(1) commonly agreed-upon beliefs that move all parties toward basic theological purposes for the church;

(2) personal character and commitment among leaders of the church which demonstrate these theological purposes;

(3) trust by members and leaders of the congregation in the character of leaders to complete tasks that maintain the basic purposes of the faith; and

(4) the pastor's inner hospitality to leadership by many persons in the congregation, and the practice of a leadership style that enables many persons to participate in a consensus.

Finding Foundation Stones

Does the church served by Pastor Reese have a solid foundation with which resistance can be respected and conflict become redemptive?

An answer to this question leads us back to the images of conflict in Jesus' parables. In the sixth chapter of Luke, Jesus refers to the storm that breaks upon two houses, one built upon sand and another founded upon rock. It is clear from the parable that the strength of a congregation during conflict is the dependence of all the people upon foundational beliefs and commitments.

Our foundational beliefs are expressed in two ways: Goals for life and ways of living that enhance these goals.

Ways of living through ultimate values are expressed by Pastor Reese in his concern for evangelism and by Zeke in his concern for worship. If the district superintendent were to lead Pastor Reese toward some basic insight on values, Reese would probably say that the concern for evangelism is a way toward salvation. This is the basic value of his ministry. In a similar mood, Zeke might reflect upon the purpose of worship, which would be the realization of God's redemptive love in our life. He would also claim salvation as a primary value.

If the pastor and his associate could speak together about their basic values, they might find a common ground of agreement in their theological commitment, which would presumably embrace both the salvation of individuals and their growth as disciples who are increasingly aware of God's love. There still would be some difference between the two leaders in terms of the priority of worship or the priority of missions and evangelism, but at least there would be some common ground within which the values of each person could be honored.

When we seek some priorities in our way of attaining ultimate goals in life, we must challenge each "contender" to express those beliefs that are most dear. The superintendent might ask how Zeke practices God's love to which he is committed. Does Zeke receive such a vision of God in worship that he can understand and obey Christ's command to honor others above himself? If he can do this, he can reduce aggressive moves into church programs that formerly were centered around evangelism and missions. He might also become sympathetic with the pastor's anxiety over Zeke's influence upon temporal sources of security for both men, which is the finance committee and the wives of some of those committee members.

In a similar way, Pastor Reese might be asked if evangelistic witness includes the way in which he relates to his church staff. Perhaps he could reread Ephesians 2 and see that salvation not only breaks down the wall of hostility between human beings and God but also reduces the barriers between people so that they are fellow citizens in God's kingdom. Does Pastor Reese have a vision of salvation that includes the assistant pastor, the education director, and the music director as "fellow citizens"?

All of these questions flow from a high valuation of theological belief and commitment to them. If church leaders and members of the congregation are not organized around this kind of basic commitment, then conflict may be irremediable. Without some common purpose, the Holy Spirit cannot become known as an agent of reconciliation in a divided staff or congregation.

The Calculated Risk of Character

In some cases of conflict, there seems to be no commitment to theological beliefs. Instead, competing power groups attack each other until the church is torn apart.[1] The emerging differences between Pastor Reese, Zeke, and others will not be resolved in Christ's Spirit unless their character and commitment express the theological beliefs that are foundational stones for church management.

Reliance upon character and commitment is a calculated risk. We seldom know the true foundations of any person apart from crisis experience, such as a church conflict. Of course, this adds to the redemptive quality of the conflict, for it is an opportunity for us to affirm what is most deeply believed among us. But it is also a very hazardous time—first, because of the particular beliefs that may be manifest and, second, in the way in which they are made known.

So far as the basic beliefs are concerned, the conflict will show faith, hope, and love in one leader. In another, there will be a mixture of these ultimate virtues with some of the deadly sins mentioned in the fifth chapter of Galatians, such as envy, jealousy, and hate. Or we may find the church leader is primarily interested in self-power or secular advantage without reference to Christian goals.

Then there is the problem of putting our beliefs into practice. Some people may be quite committed to principles of Christian living but speak too bluntly, make premature judgments, withdraw from conflict, or hide in a defensive group.

The importance of our way of virtue is strongly presented in the "fruit of the Spirit" (Gal. 5). Many of these virtues, such as longsuffering, patience, and kindness are "instrumental" virtues. They refer to our way of life, our manner of relationship, the way we express ourselves to one another, and how we carry out the more foundational virtues of faith, hope, and love.

If Pastor Reese would think about character when he talks with Joyce and Mabel, he may find a resource for the resolution of conflict between himself and Zeke in their grace, clarity, and love of the common good. Or he may find divisiveness, pride, and intolerance in these people. He really will not know until he faces them during a crisis. This is the calculated risk.

Why should Pastor Reese take such a risk? Because this is the way to maintain openness to God's Spirit through which love may be shown incarnationally. The foundational beliefs of a Christian fellowship are not expressed primarily through organizational structures or institutional hierarchies. They are made known through the ways that people relate to one another.

Some pastors do not wish this dependence either upon the Spirit or upon the Christian character of other leaders. To reduce risks, now and in the future, they spend more and more time on the organizational framework that will insure conformity and smother differences. Sometimes, they seek to do this by retaining all decision making for themselves. At other times, there are obsessive maneuvers to reduce all problems to a set of procedures that guarantee preconceived results.

Faithfulness Despite Difficulties

Does this emphasis upon character reduce the importance of organizational structure? The district superintendent accuses Pastor Reese of saying yes by default. The pastor has grown increasingly despairing and indifferent to the relationships between staff members, so he no longer meets with them. In this way, he also avoids a recognition of his contempt for fellow servants of Christ. He also seems to have narrowed his institutional involvement with the congregation into personal conferences or occasional meetings with the finance committee.

The unhappy result of this despair and withdrawal is a faithless leadership. In the face of difficulty, the leader has dropped some of the essential tasks of a church manager.

This is a violation of trust and is feared more than almost anything else by lay leaders when they are asked about their expectations of a pastor. In contrast, the Readiness for Ministry study by the Association of Theological Schools found that the laity placed the highest confidence in a pastor who was willing to complete the mutually agreed-upon tasks of his office despite a variety of difficulties.

Trust among people develops out of faithful relationships. A challenge for Pastor Reese is to call upon his years of service with the congregation, his hours of counsel with individuals. This is the stabilizing power for open discussions about differences. If he does not use this resource, then his conflicts with the church staff and others will deplete his potential for continuing ministry. This may be what he senses in his question to his old friend about the possibility of another assignment. He knows that he lacks faithfulness and courage for present difficulty and hopes that another position will reduce his responsibilities into one-to-one encounters. But this is an illusion. Although he may actually be correct in his need to withdraw from the pastorate because of personal inadequacy, he will still face the requirement of faithfulness in a counseling office. He will need to be as consistently available to people in personal distress as he should be to his congregation and staff in a time of conflicting values.

Power in Many Places

If Pastor Reese calls upon the resources of his trustworthy relationships with people in the past and develops personal courage for honest discussion in the present, then he may move toward resolution of some of his conflicts.

But will he make this move in a spirit of humility and openness to varying points of view? And will the finance committee, their wives, Zeke, and other staff members meet him in the same spirit?

Pastors who feel inadequate about themselves are unsure about their position or frightened by this question. They feel that any sharing of power with others during a conflict is an admission that they are being defeated. They fear the possibility of an answer to problems that is different from their own convenience. But there can be no Christian resolution of conflict without the humble sharing of ourselves with the body of Christ.

What will be required of Pastor Reese and others if they are going to respect the power of many people in the solution of present difficulties? A part of the answer is in the individuals. Pastor Reese would need to admit his anxiety about the rise of other values besides mission and evangelism in the changing goals of the congregation. He will need to confess to some people his uncertainty about respect for his guidance and the way in which he has served as an administrator. And he will need to express an openness to a solution to difficulties that he has resisted, which is to continue meetings with his staff and open discussion of policies, procedures, and programs with those who bear the burden of administration with him.

A similar spirit of humility and openness will be necessary for those who are going in directions that are contrary to the pastor's emphasis. Can Zeke admit his satisfaction in the development of a worship program and his contempt of the pastor's emphasis? Will he respect missions programs along with worship programs for the young people? Can he share power among several church emphases?

What about the feelings of the finance committee and relatives? Will one of them admit that the pastor has been too dependent upon their resources and guidance for the congregation? If not, can the pastor or Zeke admit this and restructure the flow of power in such a way that the chairmen of many committees are responsible for policies, procedures, and the implementation of programs in the church? This will require some difficult administrative decisions. Basically, money in the hands of a few wealthy men has become the basic source of power for the pastor and for the church's program. Is this to continue? If it does, then what is to prevent another ambitious associate from capturing the attention of these powerful people while the pastor seals himself off from his staff? To continue the present dynamics of this organization is to invite irremediable conflict.

Stop Running Red Lights

Would Pastor Reese be willing to recognize and develop all these resources for conflict resolution? The answer depends on how seriously he views the present difficulties. Although he is in despair, uneasy, and asking questions about a transfer, he might still talk himself into thinking that nothing is "really" wrong. He might tell the district superintendent that no extensive analysis of the situation is necessary and that a few adjustments in his own schedule and the staff will take care of all problems.

Conflicts cannot be resolved unless they are openly identified. So far, neither Pastor Reese nor Zeke have told the district superintendent or anyone else that a major battle is shaping up. They are on a collision course, but so far, they have used denial and withdrawal to prevent a confrontation.

How could these staff members and other church members recognize differences in values and ways of leadership that are disruptive? [2] The staff and the lay leaders need to recognize the "red lights" that they are constantly running. Some of these danger signals have been described by a management consultant, Charles A. Dailey. He identified eight warning signals for any church, beginning with the least serious and going to the most serious: (1) voting patterns indicating the rise of opposition to the leadership, (2) direct protest of a policy or decision, (3) change in attendance at meetings, (4) change in revenue, (5) a persisting issue of abrasive quality, (6) withdrawal of support by some of the power structure, (7) increase in polarization, and (8) withdrawal of key persons or groups from communication.[3]

The district superintendent or some other trusted friend might help the pastor or members of his staff to recognize these danger signals. Pastor Reese might also help members of his staff express their concerns with a series of meetings in which there would be a growing opportunity for free discussion. This was the method chosen for a church in conflict, Dumbarten United Methodist Church in Washington, D.C. An outside consultant began to meet with key members of the church in a search for mutual goals. One member noticed something about the pastor which was different from the way he had operated in the past:

> He set it up and emphasized that every person's opinion was important. This was a new attitude and technique. We didn't nit-pick. Everything anybody said was put on the newsprint (large pieces of paper on the walls for displaying goals decided on by groups in the consultation). The consultant gave us a way to have our say.[4]

A year later, several members saw more of this change. One wrote: "We have stronger leaders now who don't see this church as a one-man show. [The pastor] used to be threatened by anyone who took a leadership role. Because he knows he has been so successful, he is more relaxed."[5]

The Closed-Minded Contender

This prudent approach to conflict will work if there is Christian character among the leaders. Unfortunately, the conflict may be irremedial if the pastor or staff or some leaders in the congregation are implacable in their opinions. These closed-minded persons do not see a situation as it really is but only as they believe according to preconceived ideals.

To make matters worse, the closed-minded persons may be essentially self-serving. Any decision for the church is seen as an extension of their power or the loss of it. There is no concern for the common good, only a desperate attempt to look good in the eyes of others or feel correct in their own opinions.

Closed-minded and self-serving attitudes must also be identified along with administrative issues that can cause conflict. As we have seen earlier, conflict of values may develop either around foundational virtues of faith, hope, and love, or around the way in which we seek to implement these virtues in daily life. The same would be true for a clash with such deadly sins as pride, covetousness, and envy. The way in which these sins are carried out is as devastating as the sins themselves.

How are we to identify the attitudes that cause conflict in themselves and that destroy any realistic attempt to resolve difficulties? In the Readiness for Ministry study, there were several questions about a minister's attitudes that would cause a major handicap in the pastorate. Most of them came under the general category of "a minister who avoids intimacy and repels people with a critical, demeaning, and insensitive attitude." [6]

The presence of these difficulties in pastor, staff, or church leaders is a warning against manipulation programs as a means of resolving church conflicts. Some changes in the formal structure of communication is certainly necessary, such as regular staff meetings, but these are secondary to the more basic difficulties of personal attitudes and relationships.

When we recognize the seriousness of the attitudes that have just been enumerated, we openly declare our dependence upon the Holy Spirit. Without the acknowledged power of Christ's Spirit in his body, there can be no real healing of conflict.

In fact, in some churches, we may recognize administrative conflict as a sign of the un-Christian attitudes of leaders. The large and small fights in such congregations are the death throes of a body that no longer depends upon the spiritual head, the cornerstone, which is Christ Jesus.

What Do We Do?

When we have recognized the red lights of administrative conflict and admitted the possibility of unfruitful attitudes in our own lives, or those of others, then we can bring together the necessary resources for resolution of conflict. But what is the actual procedure by which this may be done in an organization?

1. Seek divine guidance for an awareness of Christian goals for the congregation. Through the process of prayer, personal sharing in devotional exercises, and individual meditation, we can be filled with a spirit that transcends the different goals of leaders and reduces our defensiveness to one another. We not only will receive prudence and wisdom through the surrender of our minds and wills to Christ, but we will also receive the prophetic gift of speaking the truth in love and self-control.

2. Agree on a process for conflict resolution. Speed Leas and Paul Kittlaus presented this as the first element in their recommendation for the resolution of church fights. In this process, give each side an opportunity to speak fully. Arrange a time for listening to one side and to the other, with some clarifying remarks by a consultant or leader who has an understanding of both points of view. Try out some vote on a recommended plan for action whenever there needs to be some clarification of understanding. Concentrate on specific issues of conflict and prohibit long speeches that may contain many accusations and exhibit self-serving attitudes.

3. Agree on some way in which a decision rule is to be accepted. For example, leadership may agree that a 70 percent majority vote is sufficient to resolve an issue, or they may decide that a key issue without 70 percent support will go to a small group of representative leaders. The leaders are to continue in prayer until a time when all minds are clear as to the leadership of the Holy Spirit. Sometimes the leadership decision may be a bargain; the one group will stop an annoying practice if another group will stop something else that is causing conflict.

Whatever the decision rule may be, a group of leaders must be firm about this before there is any congregational time for debates and speeches.

4. Agree on goals. The object is to see what people can agree on as well as to identify disagreement. In the Dumbarten church, newsprint was put on the walls so that leaders could write out all that seemed important to them. Everyone went around the room to identify goals and, in the Dumbarten church, found more common ground than they had formerly assumed.[7]

When this process is successful, participants testify to their new understanding of the church as an organism. It is more of a living thing than a static organization. People and groups now live in the same way a body grows, decays, fights off disease, or takes on new life. With this perception of the *body* of Christ, the congregation is better prepared for future stress. Those who press on with new programs and those who resist in the name of all that is holy to them will have common respect and commitment. There are differences in gifts and maturity, but all have a place of honor in service to the same Lord (1 Cor. 12:4–14:5).

LUECKE

Dealing with Conflict Before or After

Pastors usually do not feel confident dealing with conflict. It is typically near the top of any list of administrative concerns they want help with. Yet, conflict is inevitable in human affairs. Clearly, how to deal with conflict is a necessary skill for any pastoral administrator.

Conflict is inevitable because people are motivated by many different needs. Even when their interests merge enough to join together in some common cause, the diversity of the rest of the needs they act on still continues. As noted in the previous chapter, this fact seems to describe redeemed Christians in fellowship, too.

To hear pastors talk about it, conflict is such a worry for several reasons. It can be personally and professionally very threatening, as Pastor Reese is experiencing it. This is an obvious practical concern. But pastors' reactions often carry a tone of surprise and disappointment when conflicts arise in a church. They reflect a theological concern. It is as if they assume that, of all places, serious conflict should not appear among God's people who are one in the faith.

Pastors who want to take their administrator role seriously need first to disabuse themselves of a naive idealistic theology. Conflict is rooted in the diversity that God himself creates. That people bump into each other as they pursue different things is a condition that results from the fact that they were created with different needs. Diversity itself is not sinful. But it certainly fuels sinfulness through the misunderstandings, insensitivities, and selfishness of imperfect natures coping with differences. In giving us new life in Christ, God forgives our old sinful nature, but he does not remove it, not in this world anyway. Since even the best of Christians remain sinners, careful administration of their life together is all the more important.

There are two basic approaches toward dealing with conflict. One is to react to it intelligently and nondefensively *after* it arises, trying to find accommodations that keep the parties together despite their differences. This is a *reactive* style. The other is to head off conflict *before* it arises. This can be done by purposefully defining and structuring relationships before participants enter into them with their personal differences. Emphasis on this alternative can be called an *anticipatory* style.

Southard works with the first approach. It is particularly well suited to support-oriented leadership. The pastor or any other leader does not presume to lay out the authoritative course for others to follow. Rather, the conflict is faced squarely and openly, the different positions are recognized, and the feelings of the participants are respected so that the causes of defensiveness are lessened. When everyone feels such support, they can reach beyond what separated them and together use their best thinking to develop new relationships that accommodate the diversity they have grown to appreciate better.

In effect, this approach concentrates on helping the participants in conflict open up and become better, more mature, and more loving people. This is essentially what Southard prescribes for Pastor Reese. As an insecure senior pastor worried that he is past his prime, he especially needs to feel support. Unless he is able to share his needs, he is likely to do some foolish things.

I affirm such efforts to resolve conflict after it has arisen. As an administrator, I spend much of my time practicing such supportive techniques. Yet, there is the other way. As an administrator who is task oriented, I also find myself looking for ways to structure tasks and relationships to minimize conflict before it occurs.

Each approach has something valuable to contribute. Knowing when to use which is an important administrative skill.

Aiming for Integration When Facing Conflict

The real issue when facing conflict is how to bring about more of its opposite. The understanding of the opposite has an influence on how conflict is managed. Peace is one way of looking at it. Developing integration is another.

Peace making is of course a most worthy biblical theme. It places an emphasis on working for reconciliation between people in conflict. The values and techniques for bringing about reconciliation are essentially reactive and are very appealing to a supportive style of leadership, as reflected by Southard's approach. But from my perspective, peace remains a partial answer to the desired outcome. It emphasizes the absence of negatives, or the containment of conflict. Reconciliation does not reflect well a movement toward something more than a condition left after differences are resolved.

That something more I prefer to see is integration. This outcome implies a sum greater than its parts, a condition more positive than the absence of negatives. The biblical concept is unity, a oneness in the Lord. St. Paul wanted to end the conflict that had arisen among the Corinthians when he gave the fullest exposition of his great theme of individual believers functioning as one body. But he went on to use the conceptual base for urging greater love and service for the common good. The main point was, through diversity, to strive to build up the church (1 Cor. 14:13). As he told the Ephesians, build up the body of Christ until we all reach the unity of faith (Eph. 4:12, 13).

How to develop greater unity out of diversity is the administrative task to keep foremost in mind when facing conflict. Conflict is diversity that is not integrated yet.

Better organization is one way to develop fuller integration. It focuses on the structure for relationships, the patterns of interaction among participants who are trying to do something together. The improvement of structure cannot create the desire for unity, but it can facilitate growth in that area. Fuller integration is the payoff for all the administrative work that goes into getting something better organized. This outcome appeals to me with my inclination to pursue building tasks in the church as fellowship through the church as an organization.

In simplest terms, to organize is consciously to decide how to separate things that are confused and how to get them back together in better relationships. This process is sometimes called specialization and coordination. In current management literature, it is frequently discussed as differentiation and integration.[8] Organizing is the process of recognizing differences in the parts and then establishing the most important connecting points that will bring them back into a whole, or will integrate them.

Out of this definition comes an answer to how to cope with confusion and conflict in the church. Improved integration—and reduced conflict—will come as a church learns to make more careful distinctions among the parts and to shift emphases in the relationships that are supposed to hold them together.

Then the question is whether organizers should rely on everyone having to find new distinctions and linkages together in the midst of conflict already pulling them apart. Or should organizers draw on lessons from the past to propose ahead of time patterns of interaction that participants can use to fit their diverse efforts together and to avoid letting conflict overwhelm them? Both lesson plans are valuable, but I am emphasizing the second here.

In this case, Pastor Reese seemed blind to many of the differences that had already come into existence in the working relationships of his church. He carried a rough notion of integration in his mind, but it no longer squared with reality. His inclination was simply to expunge the parts that did not fit, as he had done with the relatively powerless educational director. But the ordained associate pastor and his powerful friends on the finance committee could not be easily sacrificed to preserve his narrow version of integration. With strong new differences and weak existing linkages, he faced serious conflict. A new integration seemed to be forming, but he was the part that did not fit so well anymore.

Since unanticipated differentiation has already appeared and will not easily go away, Reese really has little choice but to manage the conflict with reactive thinking, cautiously inviting the participants to join him in finding new, more effective linkages. Southard outlines how he might do that.

Now, assuming that he is able to keep everyone, including himself, together, what can he do to head off more conflict in the future?

The Anticipatory Approach

Anticipatory thinking could help him build better integration in the various working relationships he is concerned about. This would consist of defining ahead of time the different positions in which participants are acting as part of the church organization, along with the responsibilities and authority one can expect to have associated with each position. In other words, the *intended* organizational differentiation should be described as thoroughly as necessary. So should the *intended* relationships and rules for interaction that will help assure coordination. Ultimately, some sort of hierarchy of authority needs to be recognized before further action occurs to provide an orderly, less energy-consuming way to resolve differences that persist within the intended framework. Such forward-looking arrangements are basic to the bureaucratic model of organizing.

Actually, this anticipatory, bureaucratic approach is likely to evolve quite naturally out of reactive, after-the-fact organizing. Its main appeal is that it does conserve energy and reduce the chances of conflict. These become attractive advantages to people who have important things to do and want to see their efforts fit together. The main prerequisite to effective anticipatory integration is that the participants accept the outline of intended limits, relationship, and authority as meeting their overall need for unity. They are most likely to do this after repeated experiences of the pain and effort that go into overcoming the confusion and conflict that emerge in the absence of such understandings.

A major obstacle to implementing an anticipatory approach to conflict reduction is the amount of time, energy, and forethought required to set it up. This involves not just the mental effort of thinking abstractly about intended differentiation and coordination before they occur. It also includes all the effort necessary to win acceptance of these intentions by those who will participate. Such planning is pure administrative work.

Pastors who do not invest time and forethought in their administrator role will predictably have difficulty with the anticipatory approach. They may try using it too late—after the conflict is heating up. That is when they need to think reactively. Or they may find that it does not work even when they think out a structure ahead of time, because they did not invest energy in processing their intentions with others enough to acquire their assent to the coordinating relationships before they are needed. Then the structure itself becomes a source of conflict on top of whatever else is going on.

The administrative issue is whether to invest some time and energy on the front end, before conflict occurs, or to invest perhaps even more later after it emerges, with all the heightened feelings that go with it.

Where conflict is most predictable is a good place to make the front-end investment. This is where anticipatory thinking makes sense.

The most predictable occasions for conflict arise from limited resources. People who otherwise share much in common develop tensions when they see themselves having to compete for something they cannot all have to the measure they want it. In churches, space is limited, and many battles have been fought over who has first claim on the fellowship hall. Time is limited, and hard feelings often develop over whose needs should receive the pastor's time or whose worship preferences should be met during the prime Sunday hour. And of course, money is limited. How it is spent unavoidably reflects choices that leave some members less happy than others.

Much of the conflict Pastor Reese experienced stemmed from limited resources. Ordinarily, a reasonably secure senior pastor should rejoice that an associate is doing effective ministry that pleases members. The most apparent rub came when Zeke's activities started diverting money and membership time away from Reese's interests. Rather than to missions, more money was going to wages—for Zeke and for a seminary speaker. Zeke's retreat was diverting the youth away from the one Sunday that was supposed to have a unified emphasis on missions.

While these differences are undoubtedly symptoms of deeper tensions, there was a relatively simple way to reduce the conflict that is becoming visibly destructive. This is to anticipate such allocation decisions, to identify the conflicts early, and to clarify the authority for finalizing choices. Such deliberate planning results in an authoritative budget and calendar. Budgets and calendars are basic management tools for dealing with conflict. Leaders who invest little administrative effort on this sort of front-end activity often wind up paying for it with later conflict.

Dealing with Diversity Carefully

If conflict is rooted in diversity, why not deal directly with the differences themselves which people bring with them into fellowship life? Then there is less need to anticipate conflict, let alone react to it. Differentiation necessitates integration. The less extensive the differentiation, the less attention has to be paid to integration.

There are good reasons to try to limit diversity that make solid administrative sense. They have to do with preserving a fellowship, conserving its energy and resources, and assuring future fulfillment of past covenant commitments. But there are also good reasons to encourage diversity that are administratively important. They have to do with stimulating and renewing energy and with facilitating the arousal of new commitments. Both purposes have to be kept in mind when selecting approaches to dealing with the conflict that comes with diversity.

The earliest church would have had a lot less conflict if it had stayed simple, that is, relatively undifferentiated. Had the very first group of Christians remained only an Aramaic Jewish community, there would not have been the tendency to overlook the Hellenistic Jewish widows. The apostles had to bring special administrative control to bear on the food distribution to reduce the options for giving preference. It was the later mixing of Jewish and Gentile customs that caused so much trouble in Paul's churches. The practice of so many diverse gifts threatened to break apart the Corinthian church. The preservation instinct was strong in Paul as he tried to bring limits to emerging differentiation, urging that everything be done "decently and in order."

Yet, without such differentiation, the church of those first believers could not have had the vitality that turned it into a world religion with countless churches. We are thankful the leaders of the Jerusalem church were unsuccessful in trying to confine Christianity to a relatively simple Jewish community. We rejoice at the wisdom Paul had in respecting the diversity he faced and in the care he took to refrain from imposing limits that were too rigid.

The anticipatory style of conflict management places the emphasis on limiting diversity. This approach seeks to bring clarification and agreement to those activities, relationships, processes, and claims on resources that a group intends to support in their future interaction. By implication, others will not be supported. Leadership attention is then focused on preserving the covenant-like agreements—large and small—by discouraging unanticipated differences that could conflict with those accepted intentions. They become unwelcome distractions, to be shut out by appeal to authority, if necessary.

Preserving unity, assuring fulfillment of commitments, maintaining continuity—these are basic church values associated with efforts to limit diversity. Careful stewardship of resources is another. They can all be practiced especially well by the organizing techniques that define the limits of what will be accepted and thus reduce the occurrence of conflict. Two modern words reflect these values and translate them more directly into the organizational context that is of special concern to administrators. They are efficiency and effectiveness.

Efficiency is a term that focuses on resources. Resources are used efficiently when they are kept on target to achieve the purpose set out for them without being wasted or diverted. In this sense, good stewardship strives for efficiency. Too much diversity can reduce efficiency. Pastor Reese was worried about the inefficiency of wasting the effort that goes into a missions emphasis week by missing the youth who would be away on a retreat. This is an appropriate concern that can be addressed through the control of better scheduling. The new ideas that the staff were discovering threatened to divert church time and funds from prior commitments that still seemed important. The time spent coping with ever-emerging staff differences certainly diverted energy away from the delivery of basic intended services. For the sake of good stewardship and efficiency, the common-sense approach is to plan out well ahead of time what will be done when and by whom and then to limit departures from that plan.

Effectiveness is a term that describes how well a goal has been achieved. All organizations, including churches, have to operate with a variety of goals. But there need to be limits, if effectiveness is a concern. The more goals that are pursued, the less likely it is that any can be achieved well with available resources. Interests that become more diverse often have the result of unintentionally adding goals or changing the targets for joint effort. It is certainly reasonable to resolve differences about which goals are most important before resources are committed and conflict arises because they are not adequate. This can be done with an anticipatory approach that prescribes the authority for setting priorities. Designated authority is used well when it conserves energy for the sake of effectiveness.

For all of its strengths, however, there are dangers associated with too much reliance on before-the-fact limitations of diversity and avoidance of conflict. While preserving energy, this can also shut off the generation of new or renewed energy for participation. Increased energy for common effort comes when individuals find new and better ways to fill personal needs through the church.

As their needs and insights change and become different, what they do with enthusiasm is also likely to change. While the potential for conflict is not far behind, the potential for fellowship growth, as well as personal growth, lies ahead.

When God is at work in the hearts and minds of his people, he has a way of pushing them beyond previously accepted limits. The Spirit does work through the procedures and agreements a community adopts to guide their dependence on each other. But he continues to work on believers one by one, creating new insights, new personal interests, new particular expressions of response— leading them into greater independence. How God moves among his people—separately as well as together—cannot always be predicted. This sort of differentiation is a precious gift. It needs to be respected and encouraged. Out of these divinely inspired independent responses to God's call comes the fundamental human source of energy for church life. The danger of avoiding conflict by excessive limitation of such diversity is that, over time, the fundamental vitality of a fellowship will be smothered.

In Pastor Reese's church, there were signs of increased vitality, and new diversity seemed to lie behind it. Some of this had been anticipated and organizationally controlled, although clumsily at the expense of the education director. Her effort to differentiate curriculum by age probably had more potential for aiding personal growth than was realized. But the new interest in worship and liturgy, as experienced by several families, was not anticipated and apparently not welcomed by the pastor. And the people most interested in missions wanted a new emphasis with more social action that conflicted with the accepted approach. If Reese had known how, he could have administratively headed off those conflicts with more carefully prescribed procedures and authority that could have treated those ideas as distractions and prevented them from being considered. But should he want to do that? He would be more comfortable and the church would avoid strife. But would the fellowship have renewed energy to continue growing in the Lord?

The possibility that God is at work in the changes that bring new differences raises the importance of the reactive style of dealing with conflict. This approach stresses respect for new ideas and interests, even when they do not seem to fit at the moment. The challenge is to find ways that will guide the participants out of conflict into a better fit. This means letting the conflict happen, facing it squarely and openly, and trying to help those involved learn more about themselves and their life in Christ. Organizational efficiency and effectiveness may suffer in the process. But when done well, reactive conflict management can lead to a new integration with even more resources and energy for future commitments.

Preserving past agreements while facilitating new ones is difficult work. It means dealing very carefully with diversity and conflict, sometimes limiting it and sometimes encouraging it. The best conflict management is done by leaders who have the self-confidence and skill to be supportive enough to encourage diversity at the right time but also to be organized enough to avoid conflict for the right reasons.

Biblical Illustrations of the Two Styles

Some biblical illustrations may help pastoral administrators gain confidence in exercising the judgments that go into aiming for integration while respecting differentiation, using both anticipatory and reactive conflict management.

St. Paul could do it both ways.

The troubles of his Corinthian church are well known. They had differences in leader preferences, eating customs, and worship practices, among other things. Because of their diverse backgrounds, socioeconomic status, and personal experiences of the Spirit, this community of believers was highly differentiated. It is a testimony to the uniting power of the Spirit that they came together at all. Noteworthy in Paul's message to this church is that he does not really express surprise or disappointment that conflict and confusion arose. He seems to accept the inevitability of that.

As we have already seen, he was not willing to settle merely for peace. He wanted integration, like that of a body. They had it in Christ, and now they needed to rediscover it amidst their diversity. Thus, over and over again, he chides these believers for not having already found ways to overcome their disruptions. A recurring theme is: You are intelligent people, use your own judgment (1 Cor. 10:14), your minds (14:20), your own arbitrators (6:4); you can make everything fit together in an orderly way (14:32).

To facilitate growth amidst diversity, Paul offers general advice and guiding principles, and occasionally, he suggests compromise positions. All of that is after the fact. His sense of an evolving fellowship made up of reasonable and responsible individuals growing in faith called for a reactive style of integrating their relationships. He did not try to impose a manual of prescribed rules and positions that would restrict growth.

But when Paul addresses resource and stewardship concerns, he could get quite prescriptive in limiting diversity, designating arrangements that anticipated conflict and avoided it. We get a glimpse of this style in his effort to raise a special collection for congregations in need. He was anxious not only that there be good intentions but that the effort be effective in actually sending money to Jerusalem. He did not want any confusion or disappointment about meeting a commitment they had earlier made (2 Cor. 8:10). Thus, he gave a directive in the form of a budgetary rule and a schedule: set aside something on the first day of every week so that the contribution would be ready when he arrived (1 Cor. 16:2). When his travels kept him away, he explicitly assigned collection authority to Titus (2 Cor. 8).

Paul was even more insistent on heading off conflict when it came to the issue of who should and should not receive the special widows' assistance. That problem of resources' stewardship was still with the church years after Stephen's administrative work. Paul's solution sounds quite bureaucratic as he laid out rules for eligibility, specifying age (at least sixty), marital history (wife of one husband), and personal qualifications (well attested for her good deeds) (1 Tim. 5:9–11). Conservation was on his mind as he emphasized that, by doing this, the church "may assist those who are the real widows" (5:16).

The pastoral epistles in general reflect a straightforward style of avoiding conflict through carefully prescribed organization of positions and authority. Thus, we read about the "office" of bishop and its qualifications as well as the qualifications of a deacon. Here the concern for preservation and continuity was foremost. Apparently, past experience had shown that conflict could be anticipated and situation-by-situation reactive resolution, like that recommended to the Corinthians, was not sufficient to preserve unity.

By the end of the first century, it is evident that a formal hierarchy of superior and subordinate positions, characteristic of an anticipatory, bureaucratic style of organizing, had developed within the leadership cadre of elders in the various scattered church communities. The top position was that of bishop. According to the letters of Ignatius, the bishop was recognized as the centralized source of authority for formal acts of fellowship, such as celebration of the sacraments and acceptance of public vows. This arrangement thus brought desirable stability to these community-defining events.

The hierarchy provided an orderly way to prevent conflict through advance certification of authority and to resolve emerging conflict through the exercise of that authority.

We find another lesson about the choice of conflict management styles by looking at the great Old Testament organizer of God's people. Moses clearly had to wrestle with how much to rely on a reactive style and how far to go in organizing relationships and authority in anticipation of conflict. In the early months of the Israelites' exodus out of Egypt, he was quite reactive. He tried to deal with whatever people and whatever problems he encountered on an ad hoc basis. It took the visit of his father-in-law, Jethro, to point out one of the results. Moses and his people were wearing themselves out with all the effort that went into getting conflicts resolved as they arose.

Jethro's well-known advice was to design a governance structure of predetermined positions, established relationships, and known decision procedures. He described a coordinating hierarchy of rulers of thousands, of hundreds, of fifties, and of tens—leaders who would handle as much as possible at their respective levels. His design appears distinctly bureaucratic in style. Jethro caps off his advice with the prediction that by doing this, "You will be able to endure, and all this people also will go to their place in peace" (Exod. 18:23).

Reactive conflict management is very energy consuming. Perhaps modern ministers are more willing to risk personal exhaustion reacting to differences and conflicts as they occur. But how far do they want to go in wearing out church members in efforts to deal with conflicts that could be avoided by better organizing?

Yet, the total absence of conflict cannot be the objective. That would mean there are few differences left. Good administration done especially by a pastor has to respect the ever new diversity God gives his people. A reactive style will always be needed to find the accommodations that can bring new vitality and renewed energy into church life.

Summary

Basically, Southard sees conflict as an administrative challenge to help people become more self-confident and lovingly accommodating of one another. Luecke sees conflict as an organizational challenge to develop a better integration of the differentiation that makes churches stimulating and energetic.

Both see conflict in the church as natural and potentially constructive. Southard recognizes the plus especially in the opportunities that conflict provides for individuals to learn more about themselves and to increase their sensitivity to others. Resistance is a warning that can trigger more thoughtful and respectful interaction. The spiritual beliefs and the character traits foundational to covenant life become stronger when they are tested through conflict successfully resolved. Indeed, conflict is not so much to be resolved as to be made faithfully redemptive.

Luecke stresses the plus side of conflict as a reflection of God-pleasing diversity among his people. It provides the occasion to develop firmer, more growth-stimulating integration of the differences that can enrich community life. A pastor's positive attitude toward conflict will depend on how much he or she can appreciate the energy that Christians are moved to put into their different personal hopes for their church. Conflict flows from individualized commitments, and commitment gives a pastor something to build on.

Luecke made the distinction between addressing conflict before or after it occurs. Southard tends to work with conflict after the fact. His supportive instinct is especially responsive to heightened feelings, and strife brings these out. He does, though, encourage that the resolution of a conflict include provisions to avoid more conflict in the future. Luecke, too, prefers to let conflict occur and then deal with it—under certain circumstances. With his concern for task accomplishments, though, he stresses how energy can be conserved and efficiency increased by heading off conflict before it occurs—under certain circumstances. He would do this by planning structural provisions to limit and control differences among participants.

7

Communication with an Administrator's Touch

How Much to Communicate by Computer

"But pastor, would we really want to do that?" asked Frank Campbell. "I mean, something just doesn't seem right about that in a church. Sure, it's feasible all right. We have much of the data, and we could get more without too much trouble. With a little more disk memory, the programming would be easy. But wouldn't some people feel we are going too far?"

Pastor Ed Rollins was having one of his late afternoon sessions with Frank. They had been meeting now and then for over a year to talk about the ongoing computerization of the church's records. Pastor Rollins had just described an idea he had for a new computer report.

Frank was a young and bright customer representative for an established office automation firm. He had grown up in the congregation and was full of enthusiasm for serving the Lord, which he was specifically doing now as a youth leader. He was also full of enthusiasm for how advanced technology could help the church and the pastor do their work better. The church bought one of his micro computer systems a year ago. Frank had been careful to donate his commissions, so there was no appearance of a conflict of interest.

The first applications were for word processing and accounting information. Frank taught the pastor and several office helpers how to get the most out of the word processing capabilities. The treasurer and several other members joined in transferring the manual book-keeping records into a versatile accounting program. The financial system had been operating for about half a year.

"Frank," Pastor Rollins began, "last week, I received my quarterly report of my personal offerings to the church. So did everybody else. This got me to thinking. Why do we give members feedback only on their money? It could look as if that is all we care about. Why don't we expand that report and include a summary of other church-related activities we know about?"

Pastor Rollins went on to inquire about the membership record system they had started working on after the financial system was up and running. Frank had persuaded him they could do a lot more than just produce specialized lists and mailing labels. Several months ago, they had devised a way to have members and visitors register their attendance at Sunday worship, and this practice was gaining acceptance. The new data was entered weekly into the membership file. Most recently, they were trying to design a report that would help the pastor see changes in attendance patterns for individuals. They were excited about the possibility of spotting clues to where pastoral care might be helpful.

"If we asked everybody to sign in when they came to Sunday school or to one of our service projects," observed Rollins, "we would have a record of some other very important functions. We could summarize the amount of attendance for every member, say, every three months. Then when we send out the quarterly reports, they would reflect worship, study, and service, as well as financial stewardship."

"But won't that seem cold and impersonal?" asked Frank, a bit incredulous but also a bit excited. "I mean, those are spiritual things. Even though I am into computers, I would like to think there is more to my Christian life than a computer can count." Then came the additional reservations Frank reflected in the opening comments. He wondered, too, about how people would react when the report showed they had not done anything.

"I know, Frank," said Rollins. "I'm not sure either. I have been trying to think about the pastoral implications. Maybe I'm most caught up in the excitement of the things you've been teaching me. But I like the idea of reporting on more than money. It sends a better message of what we are about. Besides, financial offerings are spiritual, too. If we aren't afraid to tell people when they have contributed little, why should we back off reflecting when they have participated little?"

"Let's think about it some more," concluded Rollins. "I might bounce the idea off a few others around here."

LUECKE

Using a Variety of Message Sources

Is Pastor Rollins on to a good idea that makes pastoral sense? Or is he just on a computer binge, warping his practical judgment to chase technical possibilities?

Whatever the answer, Rollins is at least thinking like an administrator. He has recognized that his church organization is a source of many more messages than he delivers as a preacher, teacher, or counselor. Assuring that these organizational messages are not distracting is a fundamental step in communicating with an administrator's touch. Tapping the full fellowship-building potential of these message sources is the real challenge of administrative communication.

In this particular case, I would attach some very important qualifications to any encouragement to Rollins to go ahead with comprehensive quarterly reports on individual fellowship participation. They come from a concern about whether this congregation has structured itself sufficiently to allow this new dimension of communication to edify the members. Does it have a range of effective message sources to complement a mailed piece of paper with some potentially embarrassing numbers on it?

The pastoral issues here revolve around support and upbuilding. These are the issues Southard and I have been exploring throughout these chapters, and the question of communicating with an administrator's touch can help tie together some of our emphases. In his reaction to Rollins's computer idea, Southard will stress how the language a pastor uses in administrative matters can be more or less supportive to Christians who bring their particular culture and needs to congregational life. People can work together better when they are helped to communicate in an appropriately specialized language that is specific and structured.

Southard gets to structure but starts with a concern for supportive language. Even in thinking about communication, I am more comfortable starting with the structure for doing it. But I cannot stay away from support. I want to explore how administrators can structure and use a variety of message sources more effectively to support church members in joining themselves together in a fuller and richer fellowship life.

Communication that makes explicit what a church is striving for is basic. Explicitness ultimately lies not in the sender of messages but in the receiver. Communication is effective to the extent the intended receiver recognizes and accepts a message that brings about the feeling or action that was intended. It is a truism of human behavior that people learn differently. Some read words and can translate them directly into behavior. Others do better hearing words. Most are selective of the sources from which they choose to receive messages, written or oral. Many respond much better when they are shown rather than told. Some need to read, hear, or see messages repeatedly before they respond; others translate more quickly. Most are more confident about what a message means when they have the opportunity to play it back and test it out.

A truly supportive environment for communication is one where messages are sent out in a variety of forms so that each participant can receive them in a way that works best for him or her. Providing for a range of message sources in a church is a structural task that can be the special contribution of a pastoral administrator.

I want to highlight four types of communication or sources of messages within a church: (1) one-way spoken or written messages, (2) action messages, (3) informal group messages, and (4) formalized agreements. These categories are drawn from the disciplined study of organizational behavior (where 2 is usually treated as technology or action techniques and 3 and 4 are informal structure and formal structure). These are the primary environmental determinants of behavior in an organization.[1]

The first type of communication is by far the most commonly used by pastors. In preaching or teaching, the pastor delivers to all who are present a message he or she thinks is appropriate. It is almost always one way, from the pastor to others. How to do this effectively is a well-developed specialty unto itself, and I have little to contribute here. Southard's emphasis on specialized, specific language can be helpful to one-way communication, although he is administratively attracted to its use in two-way contexts.

Administrators specialize in the types of communication other than one-way messages. They involve people in doing things, and what the participants find themselves doing can become the message itself. Administrators spend a lot of time facilitating group interaction. I will emphasize the preliminary step of structuring a congregation so that groups, and therefore informal group messages, can thrive. The message that participants receive when they enter a formal agreement with others is perhaps the most unique administrative contribution to communication. It is fundamental to the covenant-shaping function of leadership.

My reservation about Pastor Rollins's use of a new computer report on individual church participation has to do with what form of communication it will be. If it is another, more sophisticated version of one-way written communication, it could be a message that is worse than ineffective and is actually destructive for a number of people. If it flows out of a context of well-received action messages endorsed by encouraging informal group messages, it has potential to be helpful. To be truly upbuilding, it should be used as an extension and reinforcement of the messages these Christians are already receiving through formal agreements they have made about their participation. More about that in a later section of this chapter.

Communicating Like Administrator Nehemiah

The kinds of communication I am highlighting are illustrated biblically in the leadership of Nehemiah. He used his management skills to lead the successful effort of thousands of exile-returned Israelites to build the walls of Jerusalem in fifty-two days. How he communicated with the Israelite community as he moved them into action is the main point here. How he collaborated with Ezra the priest is also interesting. They formed a great preacher/administrator team.

The Book of Nehemiah tells the story. When he arrived on the Jerusalem scene as a king-appointed official from Persia, Nehemiah said nothing for three days about his vision for rebuilding the wall. After sizing up the situation, on the fourth day, he simply pointed out to the leaders the problem of the ruined wall they all recognized; he described his view of God's gracious hand on this project; and he explained how they could get the job done with the resources he had already obtained through the king. Without much further ado, he challenged them to start, and they did (Neh. 2:11–18).

As the story reads, these community participants immediately (within no more than a day or two) found themselves hauling stones and beams and witnessing progress. For most of the thousands involved, the main type of communication was action messages. One day, they were carrying on their various personal routines. The next day, they were joined together out on the wall, putting the pieces together. Undoubtedly, they had questions about the importance and meaning of this effort; but, for most, the questions flowed from what they saw themselves doing, not from verbal debates about ideals. There also was not time for great debate about how to do it. Nehemiah confidently and visually showed them. They learned by doing, not by talking.

It was crucial for Nehemiah that the action messages be buttressed by informal group messages. He organized the effort so that people worked within their natural groupings. Discrete portions of the wall were assigned to individually named families or neighborhoods, and the interconnected group projects were carefully identified and preserved for the record, reflecting the recognition given to all the groups involved (Neh. 3). One can imagine the many easy, informal conversations that went on among friends and relatives, reinforcing the significance of their common effort and helping to keep up enthusiasm. Nehemiah did not presume to communicate with everyone directly. He worked through the natural group leaders and let them fill in the specifics in their own way.

When project progress was threatened by the hostile reaction of alarmed enemies in the area, Nehemiah reverted to more action messages. He had half the workers (by family) assume armed guard duty while the others built. Only after he could point to human security already in place did he provide the verbal encouragement of the Lord's protection (Neh. 4:7–18).

The next threat to the building project was internal within the community (Neh. 5). Nehemiah handled it with communication finalized in a formal agreement. Over time, those who were doing the work felt increasingly aggrieved against other members of the community. They were the wealthier ones who were helping support the workers but were charging interest in the process. (Presumably, the wealthier ones were not the laborers out on the wall either.) The issue was the interest. Nehemiah boldly confronted them over this specific behavior and appealed to their sense of community justice. But he did not end the communication when the nobles and officials agreed to give back what they had taken. He got them formally to pledge their promise with an oath. He even dramatically shook out the folds of his robe to show how people who broke this promise would be shaken out of the covenant community. When this communication episode was over, we read that the people "did as they had promised."

Ezra appears in the story after the wall is completed. Actually, he began leadership fourteen years earlier. He was the senior preacher and spiritual leader, specifically, a scribe and priest devoted to the study and teaching of the law. His leadership was very different from Nehemiah, the administrator. As he mobilized first a returning band of exiles and then all the Israelites already in Jerusalem, Ezra concentrated on their spiritual preparation of prayer, fasting, confession, and consecration of the priestly leadership (Ezra 8–10).

His main recorded contribution revolved around restoring the identity of the Israelites as a distinct community set apart in faithful obedience to the God who chose them. He vigorously verbally attacked the major symbol of unfaithfulness—intermarriage with the unchosen. He issued a compelling call for repentance and separation from foreign people and specifically foreign wives—a call so compelling that the elders were able to deal rigorously with all the individual offenders within ten months, having them send away their wives and children.

Ezra, the preacher, laid the spiritual groundwork for a community. This leadership was a prerequisite for Nehemiah's successful administrative effort of pulling the community through the wall-building project. The Israelites could work together because they wanted to be a covenant community on the move, and this motivation sprang from the confidence of their identity before God.

We can see the contrasting communication approaches of Ezra and Nehemiah when they joined in leading a reaffirmation of community intentions after the wall was completed. Ezra preached—a long one-way verbal message about God's formative actions, their unfaithfulness, and God's renewed mercy (Neh. 9). Then Nehemiah led all the Israelites in sending each other the message of a formal agreement, laying out in detail the promised community behavior to which each committed himself (Neh. 10). This covenant was put in writing and all the leaders, on behalf of their people, individually signed it with their seal. Nehemiah was the first signatory. He appreciated the communication value of a formal agreement that would constantly send messages, reinforcing the behavior the community was striving for.

Using Action Messages

We do not have to look for wall-building projects to see potential sources of action messages in churches today. Wherever Christians are doing things together, their actions are visual messages to each other. Their inactions are communicating something, too. Inaction as well as action can speak louder than words.

The leadership question of relevance to communication is whether a congregation's actions are sending the right messages. Do the messages coming from experience extend the pastor's verbal intentions for the fellowship? Does what the fellowship see itself doing communicate effectively what they are striving for? So often, these practical questions are simply overlooked because of a pastor's concentration on words. It is the administrator role that forces a pastor to deal with the realm of fellowship actions. Competent administration can more fully tap the communication potential of the source of messages.

One of the major sources of pastoral frustration with administration is the feeling that all the routine activities and projects can seem so trivial in the larger scope of ministry. These become much more significant when they are seen as a communication extension of the pulpit. Nehemiah ultimately was not just building a wall. He was showing how the Israelite community could restore its integrity. When the sons of Hassenaah put the bolts and bars in place on the Fish Gate, they were involved in an object lesson on what Ezra was preaching years before.

An observer looking at many congregations today can truly wonder whether their actions communicate what they mean. The pastoral administrative reaction to this observation is not a moralistic clucking of the tongue. It is, rather, to set about searching for better ways to express through fellowship action what the church is trying to become. The first step is, indeed, to be aware of what messages are actually sent by practice, not by words. Then new, more effective practices can be introduced where appropriate.

My favorite example of poor action communication is the Sunday morning worship of many traditional churches, like my own. This hour is the most fundamental source of action messages, because it is the featured time together, involves the most members, and is done with the most regularity. Yet, conventional liturgical services seem to be a poor vehicle for involving the participants in the sharing interaction that is basic to fellowship life. Much of the practice does not seem to fit with an intent to express and build fellowship. Of course, if this is not the pastoral intent, then these comments are irrelevant.

A worshiper in a traditional liturgical service usually finds him or herself engaged in passive, low-energy behavior with little opportunity to connect personally with anybody else, except perhaps passively with the preacher/liturgist in the front. There is almost no physical or eye-to-eye contact between worshipers, and most see only the backs of the heads of those sitting in front of them. Interaction between participants is severely reduced to joining in songs or prewritten statements that are done in unison and seldom evoke much thought or intensity. A worshiper rarely acts as an individual who takes personal initiative for a relationship. After the service, a worshiper may give polite greetings to those walking alongside or perhaps shake the minister's hand, but this happens on the way out. It is quite typically possible to "go to church" without having any meaningful contact or exchange with another person. Do such leader-shaped behaviors communicate a church's fellowship intent?

To design new liturgies is not the purpose here. To suggest some questions that could go into such design effort will help highlight the communication dimension of worship behavior. Is the fellowship that the worshipers are learning by doing the one that is wanted? Are there alternatives? Can participants better acknowledge the presence of others around them? Could they look at each other or even have some physical contact? Can more people besides the pastor be involved in expressing relationships? Could worshipers initiate interactions? Can they have a time in the service for conversation that moves beyond pleasantries and touches on personal religious responses? In short, are there better ways to connect more

Sunday morning participants in visible performance of lively fellow-ship sharing?

Similar questions can be asked about other sources of action messages that are more or less in use in customary church practices. Do educational programs encourage behavior that sends messages reinforcing fellowship sharing? Or do they remain a scarcely noticed source of more one-way verbal messages? Are there evangelism and service programs that visibly engage members in doing the activities that are verbally described as intentions? Does a fellowship spend its time talking about building the modern equivalent of a Jerusalem wall but, at the same time, communicate that the effort is not very important because nobody ever gets around to pushing the stones and hauling the beams?

Letting Groups Do the Communicating

Social psychologists maintain that group dynamics present the most powerful messages that people choose to receive and respond to. Groups can provide identity, support, and protection. The more attractive a grouping is to an individual, the more that person will behave in ways that meet the group's expectations. In fact, one could argue that ultimately all messages that affect a person's values or behavior come mediated by a grouping, such as the family, a social circle, a recreational team, or a task group. When confronted by conflicting messages, the person will heed those of the group that hold the most attraction.

People in church fellowships respond to messages from a variety of groups, many of which are not even recognized by church leaders. Some are inside the fellowship. Many are outside. Most are informal.

The variety of groups that touch believers can be good news or bad news. If most of the informal messages respect church fellow-ship behavior and reinforce it, church leaders are fortunate, and fellowship performance can evolve seemingly naturally. The church has a supportive infrastructure. The leadership task will be more difficult if there is a weak infrastructure; that is, if participants receive few messages from groups, and those are neutral. Group communication can also be bad news. The leadership task will be most difficult if the participants' informal groupings send out nega-tive messages about involvement in fellowship behavior. This is a competitive infrastructure.

Church leaders have long recognized the influence of informal groupings. Over the centuries, churches have tried to create something like total environments that reduce the possibility of competitive group messages. Monasteries and nunneries do this most effectively. Village parishes approximate it. In modern American experience, churches have provided all sorts of schools and colleges to encourage informal relationships that reinforce fellowship among young Christians.

Our elders can tell about congregational life several generations ago that provided a stable, pervasive, supportive fellowship infrastructure. Most congregations today, however, have members responding to a wide variety of informal, group message sources that are only randomly related to church fellowship and are often competitive. Such a situation may bring a figurative shrug of the shoulders from ministers. What can be done about it, besides lament the misfortune of being called to ministry in the fragmented society of this part of our century?

What can be done is to give increased attention to the administrative role of pastoring. The administrative task of shaping interactions can be looked at as turning weak internal patterns of relationships into strong church infrastructures that steadily send out a wide range of group-centered messages supportive of fellowship performance.

Pastoral administrators can do this first of all by recognizing and respecting whatever existing groups—formal and informal, inside and outside the fellowship—that do have the members' loyalties. Such respect came instinctively to Nehemiah. He sought the help of groups, not individuals. The people to whom he paid most attention were the ones acting in their role as group leaders. By winning their support, his message was passed on to many others more prone to listen to their own leader than to a visiting dignitary from out of town. This was communicating with an administrator's touch.

Pastoral administrators can reinforce groups by maintaining circumstances that facilitate group cohesiveness. The best infrastructure is made of many groups that are each cohesive. We know from behavioral studies what circumstances are associated with high cohesiveness: small size (five to fifteen), stability, similarity of backgrounds and interests, and a feeling of success, to name some. Leaders who insist on making groups large, or introducing into them people with widely different backgrounds, or imposing expectations that seem impossible are headed straight for a weak infrastructure. Ministers in particular are prone to interject such barriers, often for the best of pastoral intentions. A better approach is to encourage new groupings, not to overly challenge existing ones, especially if they are fragile to begin with.

Pastoral administrators can look for new opportunities to bring members into supportive groupings. The administrative question is, What will bring people together into fellowship-associated relationships they will enjoy and accept messages from? The possible answers are limited only by imagination. The opportunities range from small groups for the basic worship, study, and service activities, to personal growth and problem-solving encounters, to countless variations of social and recreational groupings. The starting attitude for deliberately building the church's infrastructure is to make and preserve groups, however possible. This is not where the process ends, but it has to have a start. Groups do need to be pruned when they drift from fellowship purposes or become stridently divisive. Those that continue to send strong messages supportive of fellowship life should be administratively watered and fertilized as carefully as possible.

The Continuing Message of a Formal Agreement

What kind of communication can a computer provide? This was the question we were considering earlier, while trying to react to Pastor Rollins's idea for an individualized quarterly report on fellowship performance.

Rollins was really looking at one of the most popular vehicles of communication used in today's managed organizations—weekly, monthly, or quarterly printouts or reports that summarize measures of activity in areas the organization wants to highlight. Typically, these use dollars to count what is reflected in income or expenditures, although many other things can also be counted, like people interviewed, applications received, or units produced. Many people today have experienced the shared joy or personal anxiety that the latest set of numbers can cause in an organization. Those dull-looking columns on a piece of paper can be a powerful message that affects how people feel or act.

Churches have long used such reports even before computers appeared. The treasurer's statement at a voters' assembly can reinforce complacency or stimulate a burst of energy. I have seen many a Sunday bulletin that announced last week's total offering and worship attendance and even the totals for the comparable Sunday a year ago. This, presumably, is as important to communicate as which hospitalized members are in need of prayers and where the youth are going next Saturday.

So far, I have not identified such reports with the formal agreements I previously highlighted as a fourth form of communication. This is what I most want to advocate as a message source that a pastoral administrator, with foresight, can structure into the relationships of a fellowship being built up together. Numeric feedback on activity is most effective when it reinforces behavior the recipient has already committed him or herself to perform. Otherwise, it remains just another casually interesting piece of information that comes as a one-way communication, easily ignored as irrelevant to anything in particular.

Imagine Nehemiah approaching an Israelite and pointing out that two of his five sons were among those who married foreign wives. Or picture him announcing to the assembly of leaders that the previous year, out of the whole company of 42,360 Israelites (Neh. 7:66), 23,218 were in giving units that brought a third of a schekel for the service of the temple. Conceivably, he did something like that at times, although the latter accounting feat would be difficult to accomplish without modern information technology.

We can well imagine the father reacting in a huff and pointing out to Nehemiah where he can put a piece of data that is not any of his business. Or we can see the assembly letting the shekel count float by with a yawn because the temple income was good enough. But I do not think that would have happened. The two numbers were reports on behavior all the Israelites had promised to perform in their formal covenant signed the seventh month after they completed the wall project. They all publicly agreed, among other things, not to take foreign daughters for their sons and to give a third of a shekel for the temple. This formal agreement had become an ongoing source of a message that people could not easily ignore because it had been structurally raised to a high level of consciousness. The current report could be an effective message of the day because its basic meaning had already been communicated in the agreement each could remember making.

The approach toward communication I am describing in this chapter amounts to broadening the array of reference points that people accept as relevant to guiding their Christian life in fellowship. God's word and its verbal interpretation by preachers and teachers remain the basic reference point and source of messages. Administrators can supplement this by helping a church develop the additional reference points of actions Christians see themselves doing and of attractive groups that send them informal messages. Arranging occasions where personal intentions are formalized in a commitment known to others and accepted by the individual provides yet another reference point.

Leaders who are administratively inclined become adept at arranging not just big ceremonial occasions for this purpose but also many, many small occasions for agreement between a few people here and a few there about fairly routine and mundane matters that become the nitty-gritty of life together. The occasion may be so small as a phone call where the pastor and Mrs. Smith agree that she will visit five named shut-ins next week. Much of the communication subsequent to such structured occasions serves as affirmations or reminders that extend the message, flowing from a reference point consciously established for the interaction.

In work organizations, computer printouts or any other quantitative report can elicit responses in behavior when the reader knows and accepts the reference point for the numbers. The acceptance comes from previous agreement to a plan; and in organizations, the plan is most effectively formalized as a budget that presents a quantitative summary of the participant's intentions. Budgets can become a valuable administrative tool when the effort is made to develop them as a form of interpersonal communication. They can appear as an oppressive irritant when they are used as a one-way message imposed by an administrator on others who had no chance to agree to the plan.

Pastoral Use of Formal Organizational Communication

Pastor Rollins is to be commended for spotting a serious weakness in the formal organizational communication occurring within his church. What officers choose to sanction as a formal message to organizational participants is a reflection of what the organization recognizes as important. Clearly, this church officially recognized individual financial contributions as important; the organization made the effort to count and report on this aspect of fellowship life. Participants did not see their leaders putting similar effort into looking after other dimensions that were verbally agreed to as intentions, like worship attendance or involvement in Bible study and evangelism. By such inaction, the organization was sending a negative action message, which could communicate that these other dimensions really were not taken equally as serious. A pastor should be concerned about this. If a fellowship is going to have an organization, the organization should be held accountable to reflect what they are striving for.

Nevertheless, I would not advocate that Rollins start trying to count and report on individual attendance at various church functions—yet. How people on the receiving end will interpret such messages is unclear. I do not see evidence of a reference point. There may be a way for the recipient to put the financial offering report in a performance context, but this is not evident either. Have the members of this church agreed to some specific level of activity that each will strive for? Have they made a commitment to do what they will be told they have or have not done? If Mr. White receives a report that he contributed $350, attended ten Sunday worship services, participated in no church Bible studies, and gave fifteen hours of service time in church effort over the last three months, what meaning should he give these messages?

Think of the power the messages would have if Mr. White had, indeed, earlier committed himself to worship in church at least three Sundays a month, to do two hours of organized service a month, and to make a weekly offering of $20, although, for reasons of his own, he declined to pursue his spiritual growth in church study groups. Then he would see that the fellowship formally recognized, appreciated, and honored his participation in what are important functions of their life together. The individual report would be a message that affirms and reinforces those specific personal commitments made as part of his life in the body of Christ. Properly interpreted, such messages could be good shepherding communication.

I do not know of any church that has structured itself to do all that I am describing here. Computer information-processing capacity is almost a prerequisite. So is the administrative arrangement of occasions when members can make the kind of commitments suggested. So is a corporate willingness to ask for any specific personal commitments in the first place. The latter is in itself a significant issue worthy of serious pastoral concern.

Actually, many churches do use the message source of formal agreements when they expect members to accept the confessions of faith of their church body or when they ask voters to subscribe to the church's constitution, which is one kind of covenant for guiding mutual behavior. Creeds and constitutions clarify intentions. How much of the intentions for the rest of fellowship life should a pastoral leader try to clarify? The more determined a fellowship becomes to build up jointly the body and reach for the whole measure of the fullness of Christ, the more desire there will be to extend their covenant into areas of sharing that make spiritual sense.

Of course, not all Christians are able or willing to commit themselves to the same kinds and intensity of response. This is a good pastoral reason to refrain from establishing crude reference points that ignore the diversity of God's people or force them into behavior no longer expressive of their spiritual responses. But rather than foregoing the communication value of covenant agreements, such reservations can be addressed by developing means to personalize individual commitments.

A financial pledge is a good example. A common practice in church stewardship is annually to ask each member thoughtfully to consider their personal stewardship of the financial resources with which God is blessing them and to pledge how much they can return as an offering into the body. The tithe is one standard or reference point. But most pledge programs encourage the individual to set his or her own standard at whatever level is appropriate for their own circumstances. This becomes the formal agreement by which each can assess his own performance, as he regularly receives the feedback of an individualized offering report.

At the time a church solicits such pledges, why could not the members also be encouraged to consider the level of activity they intend to contribute in other areas the fellowship wants to highlight? They could annually make a three- or four-part pledge instead of declaring only their financial intentions. The pastoral dynamics are really not any different from what goes on in a stewardship program. One practical reason why many churches do not systematically ask for such commitments is that preparation for and implementation of a pledge program becomes a major administrative effort. When done with the objective of structuring communication and not just as a ploy to raise income, the administrative effort is worthy of a pastor's serious attention.

What about the members whose performance falls short of their well-considered, recently affirmed intentions? This is, of course, between them and their Lord. But it should also be of concern to the shepherd who is caring for them. There may be obvious reasons of no spiritual significance. But a change in spiritual health may also be occurring in a soul that is drifting away from the flock. The data so carefully gathered and reported can become a clue to where a caring pastor can give support and encouragement.

In churches, administrative leadership can never be a substitute for the leadership expressed through preaching, teaching, or personal pastoral care. But it can be an extension of these functions of ministry. This is the understanding that can help pastors integrate their administrator role with the many other roles they are called to perform.

SOUTHARD

Integrating Specialized Languages

The church is a community of language.[2] People are called into the kingdom of God through "the hearing of the Word." The appeal of the church is specialized language that gives a deeper dimension to such common and life-fulfilling words as love, justice, forgiveness, reconciliation, faith, and hope. Words like *gospel, sacrament, second coming, born again,* and *liturgy* are symbols that provide identity and an explanation of the Christian life.

Administrators tend to speak a specialized language of their own. With others in the organization, they talk about proposals, budgets, assignments, schedules, deficits, and progress reports. They "meet" deadlines, "check out" things, "tighten up" procedures, and "run down" lists. Administrators are especially prone to talk the language of numbers—nine of this, 63 percent of that, and $752 for something else.

One of the reasons pastors have difficulties with their administrator role is that they are not confident integrating the specialized language of administration with the specialized language of faith. By training and personal conviction, they are much more comfortable with the latter. Administrator talk can be almost a foreign tongue spoken only haltingly. It is a shorthand that seems harsh not only for its style but especially for the substance it usually tries to communicate.

This language comes least easily to pastors who want to minister comfort and support. I doubt that my kind of pastoral administrator will ever talk "administratorese" as much as Luecke's kind. But I see the value of becoming more proficient—not with the jargon but with the pastoral substance. Communication with an administrator's touch can be especially supportive for some people and spiritually stimulating for all.

Frank Campbell and Pastor Ed Rollins are experiencing the dilemma of trying to use two languages simultaneously. They recognize that, because language is so important in the church, any change in the manner of communication will raise immediate problems. They want to add precision, range, and depth through the use of computerized quantitative progress reports on church participation. In doing this, they will threaten the communication that is already established, for the new method is unconnected with the spiritual goals of a congregation in the minds of many people and may be too closely connected to the personal commitment of individuals. People who say that the use of numbers is not godly might join with those who do not want anyone to know just how godly they are.

Both of these groups know something about the value of language in the church. One group sees the relationship of language to the revelation of God and the other knows that the language of God can reveal the purposes of the heart. But each of these groups needs something more.

For those who want to talk about God, there also must be an awareness of God's work in their own lives. They need to think about language as the process of salvation that Paul described in the second chapter of Ephesians. In that chapter, communion with God breaks down our barrier to God and our barrier to other people. Or as John Calvin stated in the first section of the *Institutes of the Christian Religion*, the knowledge of God and self-knowledge always grow together in Christian life. The pointed truth of 1 John is that we cannot say we love God if we do not love our brethren.

The other group is well aware of this dual function of godly language. They fear open, exact communication about their personal lives because this is the avenue through which the Spirit of God develops conviction of sin, repentance, and sanctification.[3] They may have read the last section of 1 Corinthians 14, in which a person enters a Christian assembly and hears the personal application of God's word to his own life. The secrets of his heart are revealed, and he proclaims his dependence upon God in the presence of all the people.

In addressing the objection of these two groups, we need to consider three essential elements of Christian communication: specialization, specificity, and structure. Structure is added by the admonition of the apostle Paul in 1 Corinthians 14. That which is spoken for the edification of all in a Christian assembly must be spoken in an orderly fashion to benefit others at the same time that a person seeks to express the message in his own heart.

When these three elements are working together, language will demonstrate the Spirit and power.

The Strength of Specialization

Conviction is described most often in the Bible as a result of "hearing the Word." This is the first element of godly communication—specialization. The function of specialization is to identify and correctly interpret the word from the Lord. It is a deliberate narrowing of interests, a focusing of attention on that which is special in Christian faith and the church. The speaking of the Lord's word is commonly assigned to apostles, prophets, and teachers—those who receive some special communication from God. Any member of the fellowship may testify, and some with special gifts of communication are set apart for the regular office of proclaiming God's word.[4]

How would specialization in language aid the discussion of computer technology in the church? At first, it would seem that the language of the Bible and theological studies would be a barrier to any other specialized language, such as the technical words, procedures, and counts used by administration.

But when we read the Bible, we soon understand "special" to be connected with "holy" rather than with "exclusive." That which comes as God's word is high and lifted up, far removed from any of the specialized interests of a nation, class, or a race. God's words are not our words, and his ways are not our ways (Isa. 40:55).

When we are filled with God's holiness that comes through the study of his word, then we can recognize the difference between the absolute importance of his specialized language and the relative importance of all the specialized languages that are spoken by human beings in the church community, class, and nation.

All these specialized languages can serve God if we admit their relative value and do not place any one above the others. This was one of the essential issues to be confronted in the Jerusalem conference. The language and ways of the Greeks were accepted along with the language and ways of the Jews, so long as both glorified God in all that was said and done (Acts 15).

But some well-meaning person may object, "We all speak English in our church, and we are just one big happy family." I am happy to hear this, but I always want to go a little deeper and ask such questions as Jesus did of those who gladly heard him in the Hebrew or Aramaic languages: "Why do you call me 'Lord, Lord,' and not do what I tell you?" (Luke 6:46). Godly communication is more than the pattern of words in a paragraph; it is power for a pattern of life. Holy communication cuts through the barriers that can be erected by our words and our culture and lays bare the essential ways in which we love or hate other people.

When we recognize the penetrating effects of godly power in personal communication, we are under conviction. We recognize the ways in which we have used words both to conceal and to reveal. The specialized language of our family, group, community, denomination, culture, and nation are both a blessing and a curse (James 3:9–12). We need specialized language in order to identify ourselves in relation to other people and yet that very specialization may deny to others the blessings that we have received from God.

The dual functions of blessing and cursing can be very subtle in communication patterns of a congregation. Those who speak the most holy language, in their own ears, may alienate those who suffer from a sense of unworthiness, failure, guilt, or sin. Those who are rich may never recognize the sufferings of the poor because they never speak to them; and those who are poor may avoid the rich in church as well as in the community and never share themselves with any Christian except their own economic equals. If Pastor Rollins and Mr. Campbell have been in the church long enough to observe the spoken and unspoken social structures, they will know how many barriers to communication are presented between specialized human groups.

Would the quantitative report of a computer print-out be one more specialized form of communication? Yes, but it does not need to belong to any one social or economic group in the congregation. Although the immediate appeal might be to the "technocrats," or "yuppies" who already have a home computer or use a business model, the benefits of quantitative information will be for every member of the congregation. The type of data that Frank and Ed want to feed into a computer will not come out as upper, lower, or middle class. So long as the explanatory print-out is plain, every member of the congregation may benefit from the information and interpretation.

But they will have to be careful about the interpretation. Here is where the requirement of holiness is essential. Whatever items are fed into the computer must be those that have some relevance for the Christian life. Whatever interpretations are made of the data must be consistent with Christian values. The purposes of the church must be entirely dominant in the use of administrative data.

The function of specialized language in the church is to aid people like Rollins and Campbell to select items and emphasize components of the church's life—interpretations that are relevant for purposes of a Christian fellowship. This deliberate selectivity and process of elimination is necessary for a common bond of loyalty to emerge from the dissemination of information.

Specificity: Decoding Divine Words

One purpose of leadership in communication is to move the meaning of language in one direction, toward agreed-upon goals of the congregation, both in terms of local mission and mission in the world. In this light, it is important for Frank Campbell and Pastor Rollins to discuss the collection of information, the identification of ideas that seem relevant to the church's mission, the labeling of opinions as relevant or irrelevant, and the narrowing of attention through the use of phrases and concepts to which the members give common consent.

There have been many critics of this process when it leads to a language divorced from the lives of church members. The

"Church in the World" movement of the 1960s and the subsequent debate over Bishop John Robinson's *Honest to God* were signs that the clergy had become overspecialized in the use of "god-talk."

The same criticism was made by Old Testament prophets who saw the emptiness of religious words and acts without repentance (Amos 5:21–24) and continued in the New Testament (Matt. 6:1–18).

More than specialized language is required. God's word must make a difference in the lives of those who hear. This is the function of specificity in the language of the church, as demonstrated in Peter's sermon in Acts 2 that is interrupted by the audience's cry, "What must we do?"

Modern studies of church leadership identify the importance of specialization and specificity. In Hoyt Oliver's study of pastoral authority, laity were asked about the source of authority for the minister that would be important for his leadership. The most frequent answers were a "personal relationship with God" and "experience with and knowledge of people." [5]

Neither of these aspects of godly communication can be effective without the other. Specialization without specificity is irrelevant. It is like the trumpet that issues an uncertain sound. Specificity without specialization is unstable and inconsistent. People cannot endure the plain truth about themselves apart from some spiritual qualities that will develop an open, trusting relationship. Jesus continually pointed out the spiritual blindness and hardness of heart in many of his hearers that prevented them from an acceptance that his words were true for them (John 5–8).

In the late twentieth century, in debates about the use of a computer, leaders like Campbell and Rollins must first explain how new technology will serve godly goals and then ask how open the membership will be to the information and interpretations that will come through the penetrating exposition of data.

The basic question to ask about specificity is trust. Campbell and Rollins may need to go through some of the thought that was basic to a research study on clergy-lay communication under the leadership of sociologist Tom Bennett. In half a dozen cities, pastors were asked to meet weekly for up to one year with a select group of laity. The purposes of the weekly meeting were to be a sharing of personal desires, frustrations, and successes in the management of the church. Each person was expected to speak with as much feeling as necessary for others to understand how this person was involved in the life of the church.

When the year had passed by, Bennett found that, in a third of the churches, pastor and laity had met throughout the year and had found renewed commitment on the part of church leaders and a sense of affirmation for the pastor. This happened only when pastor and laity were able to talk openly with each other about their feelings as people in positions of leadership. In another third of the churches, the minister was unable to talk about himself, or the leadership could not speak personally about themselves in the conferences. Several meetings were held and then attendance decreased and the attempts at open conversation were diminished. In another third of the churches, there was one meeting in which people became aware of what was expected of them. There was a "closing of ranks" against open communication, and no more conferences were held.[6]

To build trust for the use of computerized information, conferences will be needed between Campbell, Rollins, and many other leaders. This must not only include a general statement of the relationship of the print-out to biblical and theological goals for the church, but it must also deal realistically with issues of trust and distrust in the congregation. As we have already seen in the previous section on specialization, there are many specialized ways of conversing within a congregation, and any new form of communication with general appeal can threaten the status of the existing languages that are based on family groupings, social class, or ecclesiastical position. Most of all, there is the threat that data brings to commitment. Do those who think highly of themselves want to be measured by criteria agreed on throughout the congregation?

Structure: Spiritual Strength through Procedures

As conversations proceed with various church leaders, Campbell and Rollins will be effective if they can develop a set of procedures that will enhance trust and develop a realistic body of information for use by individual members and by church leadership.

A part of the structural requirement will be in the selection of items to be included in the monthly report to the congregation, in the way that this information is sent to individuals, and in the general interpretations of this data that would be made in the evaluation of programs and plans for others.

The early church set the standard for procedures through Paul's admonition that "God is not a God of confusion but of peace" (1 Cor. 14:33). Specific procedures for communication in the Corinthian church were necessary so that the congregation would be "edified." That is, all would be built up through the communication that was received from any one person.

Edifying procedures will consider both the Author and the Audience. The Word does not come to human beings without regard for our ability to hear, understand, and implement. Both the prophet and the conditions of prophecy will participate in the inspiration that comes to the hearer. With this understanding, "prophecy" is not an isolated disclaimer of difficult concepts, but a place for clarification of concepts that many need to draw near and hear. Edifying conversation is a word of prophecy spoken in the consciousness of the influence of the prophet upon others and of their influence upon the prophet.[7]

How can a quantitative report contribute to "edifying conversation"?

1. The channels of communication will be known. When there is some agreement on the type of information that is to be sought from the membership, the way it is to be distributed, and the groups that are to have access to general conclusions from the data, then the responsibility and trust will be increased throughout the congregation. The danger of filtering information through special interest groups will be diminished.

2. There will be direct lines of communication between church leadership and all members. The benefits will be both for Pastor Rollins and all of the members. On the one hand, he will know that each of them is receiving a message every month about some aspects of their commitment to Christ and to the church. Hopefully, he will not consider these to be the final indices of Christian growth but will treat them as one of the agreed-upon ways by which each member can think specifically about congregational commitment. When various analyses of the data show the significance of some items in relation to each other, then "indexes" can be developed for different types of commitment to Christ and the church. Some of these indices have been developed by denominational research studies, such as the United Church of Christ Report, *The Fragmented Layman*.[8] In this and other reports, commitment to the

church was seen as a variety of interests, some of which were primarily fellowship, some instructional, some devotional. When these interpretations can be given to the congregation both in talks by the pastor and in direct mailings, the strengths and weakness of each member can be directly assessed by that member.

On the other hand, the congregation has a direct line of communication to the pastor and church leaders in the information that they supply for quantitative analysis. Some surprising results can come through this kind of information feedback. When the First Baptist Church of Shreveport, Louisiana, made a comprehensive study of the membership, with computerized sorting of data, the results were to strengthen the importance of young married people in the congregation as leaders within the next ten years of all phases of the church. This was a contradiction to the commonly held belief that the church was under the control of elderly, conservative, community leaders who would maintain that control over a long period of time. As a result of this study, there was a shift of leadership development toward men and women in their thirties and the development of new church programs to support the church membership in that age cohort and the single, young adult cohort that immediately preceded it.

3. The direct, quantifiable data should help intermediate communication. By "intermediate" communication, I mean the way in which special interest groups in the congregation will interpret the general data that is available.

Intermediate communication is usually handled through "link pins." These are the persons who fit a clique in the central organizational system of the congregation or any other organization. In the study of one church, twenty-five men and women were in the Christian education cluster, fifty in the established church member cluster, and twenty-five in a prominent member cluster. Only 35 of the 114 members in the survey had no definable relationship to a cluster in the congregation.[9]

The procedures that would respect the value of the "link pins" would include some regular evaluation of information from the computer reports in both formal and informal meetings of church leadership and of the congregation at large. Variations on the wording of questions to the congregation and in the interpretation of items should be encouraged. The monthly conversations will soon show that any one question, even for purposes of clarification, will mean different things to different people. Also, an interpretation that would seem suitable from an indexing of items for young adults may not seem to be equally suitable for singles or adults who have just moved into the community from a different part of the region.[10]

Intermediate communication would also include the reports that are issued as a summary of findings from a month, a quarter, or a year. It is especially important for these reports to combine specificity concerning commitment to programs with general goals of the congregation that are qualitative and spiritual.[11]

The Board of Evangelism and Social Service of the United Church of Canada demonstrated in their 1967 report that an annual statement can be bright and informative. The report was widely circulated in secular as well as religious circles because of the relevant articles on many phases of Canadian life. The work of the church was explained in terms of relationships with the world that the church was to sanctify. In another report from the United Church of Canada, mission goals for the next year were explained in terms of specific programs and the cost of each of these programs. When church members saw the actual way in which their money would be used for projects of which they approved, there was a demonstrable increase in giving for all projects the following year.[12]

Intermediate communication also includes the impact of "buzz words" upon different members of the congregation. One pastor became so aware of this that he prepared a list of the words that meant one thing to him in a sermon or conversation and something else to the people who were listening and responding to him:

When the pastor was saying: The people were hearing:

- minister
- go deeper
- renewal
- fellowship
- relational

- preacher
- get busier
- revival
- church socials
- friendly[13]

4. There must be formal and continual support for channels of communication. It may seem strange for this question to be considered by Pastor Rollins and Frank Campbell, but they will soon find that some leaders do not want to make decisions on the basis of data from a computerized survey. They are much more comfortable with their own opinions as set in previous years by a

tradition with which they are familiar. And there is also the possibility that the pastor would not be pleased with the quantifiable information that is available to him concerning church growth and commitment. If both the pastor and some leaders are challenged by the data, they may easily practice "selective inattention." That is, they may use some of the information for their own purposes at crucial times in a debate, skew the information toward conclusions that are favorable to their own opinions, or neglect the data all together.

I cite these cautions from the well-known tendency of churches who neglect "self-study" program results. John Bartholomew found that the overwhelming majority of self-study reports, which were required of Presbyterian churches before they called a new pastor, could not even be found by the church leadership after several years had passed. The reports had been briefly noted by the church leaders as they were seeking to call a pastor and then completely neglected, even though a monumental amount of statistical information concerning the church and the community had been given by the report.

To be formal in procedures concerning data is to be faithful as a Christian to all aspects of the truth. This is probably the greatest question of character for leadership in use of computer technology. Will the leaders look into the mirror of themselves which they have created through their questionnaire results, or will they at once forget what they are like? (James 1:22–25). They can only meet this test through a willingness to combine the special character of Christian language that brings humility, courage, and sacrifice in combination with the specific language that reveals the quantitative results of their administration of a congregation.[14]

Summary

Communication is a good topic with which to end our dialogue. It is general and indirectly cuts across almost all the aspects of leadership we have addressed. It is of special relevance for pastors. In all of their various roles, pastors remain professional communicators.

With our differing orientations, we offer different interpretations

of the administrator's touch in communication. Southard emphasizes the language administrators use to communicate. He sees them
adding a specialized vocabulary that increases specificity and aids
the development of structure. Luecke emphasizes the forms administrators can give to communication. He sees them augmenting
one-way verbal messages with messages coming from actions, informal groups, and formal agreements.

We really have different objectives for our communication emphases. But then we started off with different objectives for the
overall work of administration. Luecke wants to teach people how
to *act* together. Reflecting his covenant-for-a-journey theme, he
works pragmatically at getting people to translate messages into
action, and he stresses messages that come from the community.
If communication from one kind of community source does not
get through, the administrative challenge is to strengthen another
kind. Southard wants to teach people how to *feel* about one another.
Reflecting his love-with-justice theme, he works clinically to use
specific specialized language that can lay bare the essential ways
we love or dislike other people. His administrative challenge is to
develop trust through the way people communicate.

Our standpoints differ, but then so do our images of who we
are as administrators. Southard stands beside the people with whom
he is communicating. He is a counselor. He figuratively has his
arm around their shoulders as they walk along. He sensitively inter-
prets information about them individually and as a church in order
to help all better understand themselves in relation to God. Daring
to be a model himself, he suggests ways to make their mutual
conversation more supportive of one another. Luecke stands ahead
of people with whom he is communicating. He is an architectural
builder. Holding out a vision of a better fellowship life with one
arm, he reaches back with the other to pull participants along in
the pursuit of it. His communication tries to grab them in as many
ways as possible. Southard stresses God's people as they are. Luecke
stresses God's people as they can become.

We both understand and appreciate the leadership function of
offering both support and structure. But we get from one to the
other differently. For Luecke, structure can provide support. For
Southard, support needs structure. We are each more comfortable
with the opposite starting point.

Task oriented, Luecke genuinely enjoys goal-directed activity for
himself; and he thrives on the task of helping others structure

themselves to achieve common objectives, particularly when those are objectives of becoming a more God-pleasing fellowship. To support other people in the way most needed at the time is one of those objectives, and all can experience individual support better when brought into relationships with others prepared to give it. Support oriented, Southard genuinely enjoys probing self-understanding, and he thrives on finding ways to help others feel loved and stimulated in their relationships with one another and God. To be more lasting and affirming under various circumstances, these relationships need the trustworthy pattern for interaction that comes from stable, just structures.

Despite our differences, we are one in our commitment to administration as a vital function of ministry. We agree in our understanding that church leadership is a larger function than can be adequately fulfilled by pastors in only their traditional preaching and teaching roles. We join in believing that the diverse contributions the ministry of administration can make are more than any one pastoral administrator can perform well individually. We are drawn together in respect for each other's strengths, even as we try to make the most out of the limited approach each feels most confident to follow. We believe pastors can combine some of both our approaches with their own personal strengths as an administrator and a pastor.

We hope our dialogue has been helpful. We have tried to highlight touch points for pastors with many backgrounds and interests. Each will have his or her own strengths, instincts, and preferences and the insights that come from them. These can be as beneficial to someone else, like a fellow pastor, as they can be complemented by someone else, like a lay leader colleague. We urge that the reader find someone with whom to continue the dialogue—someone who sees, reacts to, and thinks about leadership differently.

Notes

Chapter 1. Searching for an Integration of Management and Ministry

1. Samuel W. Blizzard, "The Minister's Dilemma," *The Christian Century,* 25 April 1956, 508–9.

2. Edgar W. Mills and John P. Koval, *Stress in the Ministry* (New York: Idoc, 1971), 57ff.

3. Samuel W. Blizzard, "The Protestant Parish Minister's Integrating Roles," *Religious Education* (July–August 1958).

4. Erik Erickson, *Young Man Luther* (New York: W. W. Norton, 1958), 115, 123, 134–35, 178–79; and idem, *Insight and Responsibility,* (New York: W. W. Norton, 1964), 132ff.

5. David S. Luecke, "The Professional as Organizational Leader: An Organizational Behavior Study of Parish Ministers" (Ph.D. diss., Washington University, 1971). Summarized in "The Professional as Organizational Leader," *Administrative Science Quarterly* 18 (March 1973).

6. James Ashbrook, "Ministerial Leadership in Church Organization," *Ministry Studies* 1 (May 1967):24–25.

7. Our distinction between task and support is an expression of findings from the mainstream of leadership research over the last forty years.

At Ohio State University, the Bureau of Business Research, beginning in 1945, sought to shift emphasis from leader traits to leader behavior. After considerable statistical analysis of descriptions of how leaders behaved, their studies identified the two major dimensions as *initiating structure* and *consideration* (Ralph M. Stogdill and Alvin E. Coons, eds., *Leader Behavior: Its Description and Measurement* [Columbus: Ohio State University Press, 1957]).

The Survey Research Center at the University of Michigan identified two clusters of attitudes that seemed to be related to effectiveness. These were called employee orientation and production orientation. Rensis Likert claimed there is evidence that supervisors with an employee orientation were most consistently effective (Rensis Likert, *New Patterns of Management* [New York: McGraw-Hill Publications, 1961]).

Out of the work at the Research Center for Group Dynamics, Dorwin Cartwright and Alvin Zander claimed two categories of group objectives: the achievement of some group goal or the maintenance of the group itself. Leadership is effective when it helps the group realize either of these objectives (Dorwin Cartwright and Alvin Zander, eds., *Group Dynamics: Research and Theory*, 2d ed. [Evanston, Ill.: Row Peterson, 1960]).

Robert R. Blake and Jane S. Mouton are organizational development specialists who popularized the two theoretical concepts in their "managerial grid," which distinguished between management attitudes that emphasized task accomplishment and that stressed development of personal relationships. Through their leadership training, they strove to develop balanced attitudes, which they featured as team management (Robert R. Blake and Jane S. Mouton, *The Management Grid* [Houston: Gulf Publishing, 1964]).

Fred E. Fiedler recognized the same two dimensions of task-oriented and relationship-oriented attitudes but, through his research, argued persuasively that effective leadership does not always come through an ideal balance of the two. An unbalanced emphasis on one or the other can be effective under certain circumstances, called contingencies, which he recognized as the needs of the followers and how structured the situation is (Fred E. Fiedler, *A Theory of Leadership Effectiveness* [New York: McGraw-Hill Publications, 1967]).

Further model refinement around *task behavior* and *relationship behavior* has been done by Paul Hersey and Kenneth H. Blanchard at the Center for Leadership Studies. They advocate a situational leadership where the amount of guidance and direction and the amount of socioemotional support depends on the readiness (maturity) that followers exhibit in performing specific functions (Paul Hersey and Kenneth H. Blanchard, *Management of Organizational Behavior* [Englewood Cliffs, N. J.: Prentice Hall, 1969]).

Recent leadership research has focused on the contingencies or intervening variables where the different dimensions are most effective. (See R. J. House, "A Path-Goal Theory of Leader Effectiveness," *Administrative Science Quarterly* 16 [1971]:321–39. See also Gary A. Yukl, *Leadership in Organizations* [Englewood Cliffs, N. J.: Prentice Hall, 1981]).

The studies highlighted have differed in focusing on either leadership attitudes or leader behavior. The first should determine the second but does not consistently do so. Behavior is the better predictor of effectiveness. But in our present writing, we are addressing the attitudes or inclinations that pastors bring to administration. Since the whole pastoral task often focuses on relationships, we choose to identify the second as support orientation as distinguished from orientation to accomplishing tasks or goals.

8. Drawn from David S. Luecke's exploration of the Leader Behavior Description Questionnaire in "The Professional as Organizational Leader."

9. Available from Learning Resources Corporation, 8517 Production Avenue, P.O. Box 26240, San Diego, California, 92126.

10. Robert R. Blake and Jane S. Mouton, *The New Managerial Grid* (Houston: Gulf Publishing, 1978).

11. Fred E. Fiedler, *A Theory of Leader Effectiveness* (New York: McGraw-Hill Publications, 1967).

Chapter 3. Why Pastoral Administration Is So Important Today

1. Emil Brunner, *The Misunderstanding of the Church* (Philadelphia: Westminster Press, 1955).

2. Jurgen Moltmann, *The Church in the Power of the Spirit* (New York: Harper and Row, 1977), 333–37.

3. Variations of these five models appear in most accounts of the evolution of organization theory. Max Weber is usually cited for offering the basic distinction between traditional, charismatic, and rational/legal bases of authority for organizing effort. The third is also known as a bureaucratic or classical theory. Beginning in the 1930s, the human relations movement was a reaction and an alternative to the classical model. Systems thinking has emerged in recent decades as an overall framework for synthesizing the other insights.

4. Peter F. Rudge, *Ministry and Management* (London: Tavistock, 1968).

5. For an exposition of Ephesians 3:10, see W. O. Carver, *The Glory of God in the Christian Calling* (Nashville: Broadman Press, 1949), 202–15.

6. See especially chapter 1, "Historicity and the Image of the Church,"

in Hans Küng, *The Church* (Garden City, N. Y.: Image Books, 1976). A New Testament scholar, W. D. Davis, found no single fixed pattern of institutional forms in the primitive church. Instead, the New Testament displayed a disciplined community with a diversity of organization. See W. D. Davis, *A Normative Pattern of Church Life in the New Testament: Fact or Fancy?* (London: James Clark, n.d.), 22.

7. See Talcott Parsons, "Pattern Variables Revisited: A Response to Robert Dubin," *American Sociological Review* 25 (August 1960):467–83; Hoyt Oliver, "Professional Authority and the Protestant Ministry" (Ph.D. diss., Yale Divinity School, 1966); Ronald Lee, "The Practice of Ministry," *Journal of Pastoral Care* (March 1972), 33; David S. Luecke, "The Nature and Function of Formal Organization in a Church" (Masters thesis, Concordia Seminary, 1967).

8. L. S. Thornton, *The Common Life in the Body of Christ,* quoted in J. Robert Nelson, *The Realm of Redemption* (London: Hepworth Press, 1964), 54.

9. Jurgen Moltmann, *Hope for the Church* (Philadelphia: Westminster, 1977).

10. The relationship of these terms in the Episcopal church has been shown by Charles Y. Glock, Benjamin B. Ringer, and Earl R. Babbie, *To Comfort and to Challenge* (Berkeley: University of California Press, 1967), 107–8, 197–98, 203–16.

11. Donald L. Metz, *Goal Subversion in New Church Development* (Berkeley, Calif.: Survey Research Center, 1966), 46.

12. Jeffrey K. Hadden, *The Gathering Storm in the Churches* (Garden City, N. Y.: Doubleday and Co., 1969), 139–40.

13. Charles Y. Glock and Benjamin B. Ringer, "Church Policy and the Attitudes of Ministers and Parishioners on Social Issues," *American Sociological Review* 21 (1956):148–56.

14. Thomas C. Campbell and Yoshio Fukuyama, *The Fragmented Layman* (Philadelphia: Pilgrim Press, 1970), 222–24.

15. The story is told in William R. Nelson and William F. Lincoln, *Journey Toward Renewal* (Valley Forge, Pa.: Judson Press, 1971).

16. For New Testament evidence and answers, see Bernard Cooke, *Ministry in Work and Sacraments: History and Theology* (Philadelphia: Fortress Press, 1976), 36ff.

17. Grace Goodwin, *Rocking the Ark* (New York: United Presbyterian Board of National Missions, 1968), 208.

18. Dean R. Hoge and Jeffrey Faue found no disagreement between the clergy and laity of the Presbyterian Church, U.S.A. on priority for preaching, religious education, and individual spiritual guidance. "Sources of Conflict over Priorities of the Protestant Church," *Social Forces* 52 (1973):181.

Chapter 4. A Personal View to Keep Administration Exciting

1. A discussion of the contending groups of strong and weak may be found in Paul Minear, *The Obedience of Faith* (Naperville, Ill.: Alex R. Allison, 1971), 8ff.

2. Glock, Ringer, and Babbie, *To Comfort and to Challenge,* 107–8 (see chap. 3, n. 10).

3. See the conclusions concerning Episcopalians in ibid., 198.

4. Ibid., 108.

5. Campbell and Fukuyama, *The Fragmented Layman,* 167 (see chap. 3, n. 14).

6. Donald W. Zimmerman and Arleon L. Kelley, *Tension: Security or Mission?* (Indianapolis: Indiana Council of Churches, 1966), 77.

7. Campbell and Fukuyama, *The Fragmented Layman,* 104.

8. The theme has been worked out psychologically in Andres Angyal, *Foundations for a Science of Personality* (New York: Commonwealth Foundation, 1941).

Chapter 5. How Administrators Can "Move" People

1. Douglas McGregor, *The Human Side of Enterprise* (New York: McGraw-Hill, 1960); Frederich Herzberg, *Work and the Nature of Man* (New York: World Publishing Co., 1966); Rensis Likert, *The Human Organization* (New York: McGraw-Hill, 1967); Chris Argyris, *Integrating the Individual and the Organization* (New York: John Wiley and Sons, 1964). For expectancy theory, see Victor Vroom, *Work and Motivation* (New York: John Wiley and Sons, 1964); and Lyman Porter and Edward Lawler, *Managerial Attitudes and Performance* (Homewood, Ill.: Richard D. Irwin, 1966).

2. Abraham Maslow, *Motivation and Personality* (New York: Harper and Row, 1954). His model is presented and discussed in most introductory texts on management.

3. Modified Houts Questionnaire, or the Trenton Spiritual Gifts Analysis, from the Charles E. Fuller Institute of Evangelism and Church Growth, Box 989, Pasadena, Calif. 91101.

4. Daniel W. Pawley, "Gifts and Growth: A Case Study," *Leadership* 3 (Winter 1982):92–99.

5. George Adam Smith, *The Book of Isaiah* (New York: Harper, n.d.), 1:191.

6. J. R. P. French, Jr., and Bertram Raven, "The Basis of Social Power," in *Studies in Social Power,* ed. D. Cartwright (Ann Arbor: University of Michigan Press, 1959), 150–67.

7. See this theme in Chester Bernard, *Functions of an Executive* (Cambridge, Mass.: Harvard University Press, 1938).

8. Elisa L. DesPortes, *Congregations in Change* (New York: Seabury Press, 1973), 153.

9. Goodman, *Rocking the Ark,* 208 (see chap. 3, n. 17). The principle of power through many leaders is discussed by Lyle Schaller and Charles Tidwell, *Creative Church Administration* (Nashville: Abingdon Press, 1975), 56–58.

10. Samuel Southard, ed., *Conference on Motivation for the Ministry* (Louisville: Southern Baptist Seminary, 1959), 73–78.

11. Zimmerman and Kelley, *Tension: Security or Mission?* 73–79 (see chap. 4, n. 6).

12. Frederich Hertzberg, "One More time: How Do You Motivate Employees?" *Harvard Business Review* (January–February 1968), 53–61.

13. Schaller and Tidwell, *Creative Church Administration,* 71.

14. John Henry Felix, *Volunteer Development: A Basic Guide* (Honolulu, 1981); see also *Leadership* 3 (1982), on the issue of volunteers. Douglas W. Johnson, *The Care and Feeding of Volunteers* (Nashville: Abingdon Press, 1978); Kenneth Blanchard and Spencer Johnson, *The One Minute Manager* (William Morrow and Co., 1982).

15. James Ashbrook, "Ministerial Leadership in Church Organization," *Ministry Studies* 1 (May 1967):24–25. In administrative literature, these items are referred to as "instrumental" leadership. They are the actual ways in which the pastor becomes an enabler. Along with this quality, there must also be expressive purposes, a statement of what the organization stands for and the motivation of individuals to participate in the task. The "instrumental" means move toward the "expressive" purposes.

16. David W. Ewing, "Discovering Your Problem-Solving Style," *Psychology Today* (December 1977), 69–73.

Chapter 6. How Administrators Can Deal with Conflict

1. For an example of a power struggle in which theological beliefs are more implicit than explicit, see "The Local Church in Crisis," *Chicago Theological Seminary Register,* June 1966, pp. 4–11. I suspect that these theological conflicts may be closely associated with the "disintegrating, dysfunctional, and dissociating conflicts" mentioned by Speed Leas and Paul Kittlaus, *Church Fights* (Philadelphia: Westminster Press, 1973), 16–17.

2. An example of prudent leadership in which at least one person recognized the difficulties was in the "Elmhurst" case reported in the *Chicago Theological School Register.* One church council member noted the growing division of the actively committed and other interested mem-

bers of the church from the professional leadership by clergy. The member called for open discussion, more flexibility in the clergy and in the leadership council, and a broader program that would have a place for all who were committed. See "The Local Church in Crisis."

3. Charles A. Dailey, "The Management of Conflict," *Chicago Theological Seminary Register*, May 1969, p. 3.

4. Elisa L. DesPortes, *Congregations in Change* (New York: Seabury Press, 1973), 82.

5. Ibid., 91.

6. David Schuler et al., *Readiness for Ministry* (Vandalia, Ohio: Assn. of Theological Schools in the U. S. and Canada, 1975), 1:7–8. In particular, laypeople identified the following problem attitudes:

(1) self-serving—often belittles a person in front of others, tends to be abrupt and impatient when talking with people, uses ministerial role to maintain a sense of superiority, is quick to condemn people whose words and actions seem questionable to him, and uses sermons to attack certain members of the congregation or community; (2) emotional immaturity—tends to be cold and impersonal, frequently shows favoritism, rejects criticisms as disrespect for ministerial office, pouts publicly when things don't go own way, and worries excessively what others think about him/her; (3) secular lifestyle—enjoys visiting local nightclubs and cocktail lounges, occasionally gambles and smokes heavily (tobacco) in public, and occasionally tells jokes that hearers consider dirty; and (4) undisciplined lifestyle—occasionally involved in extramarital affairs or illicit sexual relationships, lives beyond personal means, displays irritating mannerisms, and displays mannerisms commonly associated with the opposite sex.

7. See a summary of these ideas in Leas and Kittlaus, *Church Fights*, 56–58.

8. See especially Paul R. Lawrence and Jay W. Lorsch, *Organization and Environment: Managing Differentiation and Integration* (Cambridge, Mass.: Harvard University Press, 1967).

Chapter 7. Communication with an Administrator's Touch

1. Luecke's application of these conventional categories from the study of organizational behavior is drawn from their use in role analysis. There, the question is how participants adapt to the various roles that are evident in organized endeavors, and the answers are found in the different sources of expectations for their performance. These are typically from the role messages sent out from the individual's own personality and needs, from the groups to which the individual relates, from the technological givens in the work situation, and, only partially, from the job descriptions and

directives issued by official authority figures. While the latter often appear as an imposition of expectations, there are limits to what participants will accept, and the formal structure is best looked upon as a set of agreements by which supervisor and subordinates will abide.

For the theoretical insights that opened up those relationships for application outside a work organization, I am particularly indebted to John W. Hunt, *The Restless Organization* (New York: John Wiley and Sons, 1972). For a basic treatment of role analysis in joint effort, see Daniel Katz and Robert L. Kahn, *The Social Psychology of Organizations*, 2d ed. (New York: John Wiley and Sons, 1978).

2. See the discussion of this phrase in James Gustafson, *Treasure in Earthen Vessels* (New York: Harper and Brothers, 1961), 42ff.

3. 1 Corinthians 2:1–5. See the explanation of "persuasive" in Gerhard Friederich, ed., *Theological Dictionary of the New Testament* (Grand Rapids, Mich.: Wm. B. Eerdmans, 1975), 6:8–9.

4. This expectation of specialized communication for church leaders was emphasized in a research study of Presbyterians, Methodists, Catholics, Lutherans, Episcopalians, Disciples of Christ, and Southern Baptists by Hoyt Oliver. The first expectation of a clergy person by the laity was that he would serve as a "spiritual guide." "Pastoral Authority: Report to the Presbyterian Board of National Ministries," Atlanta, Georgia, 1967, p. 16.

5. Ibid., 18.

6. Thomas Bennett, "A Report of Project Laity," Department of the Church and Economic life, National Council of Churches, New York, 1961.

7. The philosophical background for this type of communication is Martin Heidegger's "Fieldof Being," as presented in Jules Moreau, *Language and Religious Language* (Philadelphia: Westminster Press, 1961), 66–73.

8. Campbell and Fukuyama, The Fragmented Layman (see chap. 3, n. 14).

9. This method has been used by Merton Strommen to advise individual young people and their leaders concerning the profile of the individual youth in relation to other youths and the relationship of the profile of the church youth program to other youth programs of the same denomination and other denominations.

10. For examples of link-pins and cliques in one Lutheran church, see the study by Jack Balswick and Norman Layne, "Studying Social Organization in the Local Church," *Review of Religious Research* 14 (Winter 1973):101–9.

11. An example of good practice in the subjective-objective dimension of reporting is described by Nancy Geyer and Shirley Noll in *Team Building and Church Groups* (Valley Forge, Pa.: Judson Press, 1970), 32.

12. *Canada and Its Future* (Toronto: The United Church House, 1967).

13. David Haney, *Breakthrough into Renewal*, pp. 35–36.

14. The four items used on pages 185 through 188 have been adapted from Bernard, *The Functions of an Executive*, 175–81, (see chap. 5, n. 7). Additional inspiration came from Katz and Kahn, *The Social Psychology of Organizations*, 225–29; and Gustafson, *Treasure in Earthen Vessels*. Additional material on formal support of communication may be found in Herbert Simon, *Administrative Behavior* (New York: Macmillan, 1957), chap. 8. Specific direction on simplicity and directness in report writing will be learned through Sue Nichol's *Word on Target* (Richmond, Va.: John Knox Press, 1963). Some techniques for facilitating trust through communication in an organization may be found in Chris Argyris, *Interpersonal Competence and Organizational Effectiveness* (Homewood, Ill.: Richard D. Irwin, 1962).

Bibliography

1. FOUNDATIONAL STUDIES

Church and Ministry

Allen, Roland. *Missionary Methods: St. Paul and Ours*. Chicago: Moody Press, 1959. An experienced Anglican missionary contrasts the sharing and primary group emphasis of St. Paul's missionary organization with the hierarchical and control-oriented organization of modern churches, especially mission-supported churches.

Anderson, James D., and Ezra Earl Jones. *The Management of Ministry*. New York: Harper and Row, 1978.

Avis, Paul D. L. *The Church in the Theology of Reformers*. Atlanta: John Knox Press, 1981.

Campbell, T. C., and G. B. Peterson. *The Gift of Administration: Theological Basis for Ministry*. Philadelphia: Westminster Press, 1981.

Cook, Bernard. *Ministry in Word and Sacraments: History and Theology*. Philadelphia: Fortress Press, 1976. A Roman Catholic scholar traces the relationship of ministry and service to the structure of the church and its offices from New Testament times until the twentieth century.

Dulles, Avery. *Models of the Church*. Garden City, N. Y.: Doubleday and Co., 1974. A comparison of five different models of the church, with an evaluation of each for the structure of the church of the future.

Hockendicj, J. C. *The Church Inside Out.* Philadelphia: Westminster Press, 1964. The theologian who sparked the "church in mission movement" of the 1960s provides a theological challenge for the church to move out of its security as an organization into a missionary structure that serves the community.

Hutcheson, R. G., Jr. *Wheel within the Wheel: Confronting the Management Crises of the Pluralistic Church.* Atlanta: John Knox Press, 1979.

Küng, Hans. *The Church.* Garden City, N.Y.: Image Books, 1976. A noted and controversial Roman Catholic theologian provides a systematic biblical analysis of the simple and fluid nature of the early church in which each person was responsible for the exercise of some gifts.

Lindgren, Alvin J. *Foundations for Purposeful Church Administration.* Nashville: Abingdon Press, 1965.

Manson, T. W. *Ministry and Priesthood: Christ and Ours.* Atlanta: John Knox Press, n.d. An English biblical scholar develops the theory from New Testament evidence that we are all priests to each other in the body of Christ.

Niebuhr, H. Richard. *The Purpose of the Church in Its Ministry.* New York: Harper, 1956.

Rudge, Peter R. *Ministry and Management.* New York: Barnes and Noble Books, 1968.

Snyder, Howard. *The Problem of Wineskins: Church Structure in a Technological Age.* Downers Grove, Ill.: InterVarsity Press, 1975.

Pastoral Leadership

Dale, Robert. *Ministers as Leaders.* Nashville: Broadman Press, 1984. An explanation of leadership styles. Emphasis on the relationship of leadership styles and various kinds of followers.

Engstrom, Ted W., and Edward R. Dayton. *The Art of Management for Christian Leaders.* Waco, Tex.: Word Books, 1976.

Greenleaf, Robert K. *Servant Leadership.* Ramsey, N. J.: Paulist Press, 1977.

Gustafson, James. *Treasure in Earthen Vessels.* New York: Harper and Brothers, 1961. *The Church as Moral Decision Maker.* Boston: Pilgrim Press, 1970. From a theological and sociological point of view, a professor of ethics discusses the primary relationships that undergird fellowship and decision making in a congregation.

Noyce, Gaylord. *New Perspectives on Parish Ministry: A View from the Third World.* Valley Forge, Pa.: Judson Press, 1981. A Yale professor of pastoral theology uses the experiences of developing Third World cultures to speak to the topic of revitalizing American life in the local church.

Schaller, Lyle E. *Getting Things Done: Concepts and Skills for Leaders.* Nashville: Abingdon Press, 1986. Discusses characteristics of an effective leader and demonstrates how leadership skills can be learned and sustained in a congregational context.

Schult, R. E., and Ronald Sunderland, eds. *A Biblical Basis for Ministry.* Philadelphia: Westminster Press, 1981.

Smith, Donald P. *Congregations Alive: Practical Suggestions for Bringing Your Church to Life through Partnership in Ministry.* Philadelphia: Westminster Press, 1981. From an extensive survey of ninety-seven churches known for their commitment to ministry, Presbyterian executive Smith examines the style of pastoral and lay leadership that nurtured them.

Worley, Robert C. *A Gathering of Strangers: Understanding the Life of Your Church.* Philadelphia: Westminster Press, 1976. A series of exercises is provided to enable church leaders and members to shape their lives in the church according to their diverse goals and gifts.

————. *Dry Bones Breathe.* Philadelphia: Westminster Press, 1977. From his experience as a consultant in many congregations, Professor Worley provides insight on the developing of a vital congregation; for the research that underlies this report, see Norman Shawchuck, et al. *Experience in Activating Congregations.* Philadelphia: Westminster Press, 1977.

A variety of theoretical and practical volumes are in continual production from publishers and church-management organizations. To remain current with literature in the field, request publication lists from:

Abingdon Press, 201 Eighth Avenue South, Nashville, Tenn. 37202

The Alban Institute, Mount St. Alban, Washington, D. C. 20016

Broadman Press, "Leadership Series," 127 Ninth Avenue North, Nashville, Tenn. 37234

Exploration Press, Chicago Theological Seminary, 5757 University Avenue, Chicago, Ill. 60637

Leadership magazine, Box 1105, Dover, N. J. 07801

2. OPERATIONAL ISSUES

General Overview of Applied Administration
  Applying Concepts to Practice

Anderson, James D., and Ezra E. Jones. *The Management of Ministry.* New York: Harper and Row, 1978.

Kilinski, Kenneth, and Jerry Wofford. *Organization and Leadership in the Local Church.* Grand Rapids, Mich.: Zondervan Publishing, 1973.

Lindgren, Alvin J., and Norman Shawchuck. *Management for Your Church.* Nashville: Abingdon Press, 1977.

Schaller, Lyle, and Charles Tidwell. *Creative Church Administration.* Nashville: Abingdon Press, 1975.

Tidwell, Charles A. *Church Administration: Effective Leadership for Ministry.* Nashville: Broadman Press, 1985. We recommend this as the most important book in this group.

Very Practical "How to"

Bingham, Robert E. *Traps to Avoid in Good Administration.* Nashville: Broadman Press, 1979.

Dobbins, G. S. *The Churchbook: A Treasury of Materials and Methods for Pastoral Leadership in Church Life.* Nashville: Broadman Press, 1951.

Holck, Manfred, Jr. *Clergy Desk Book.* Nashville: Abingdon Press, 1985. This book is the most beneficial.

Powers, Bruce P. *Church Administration Handbook.* Nashville: Broadman Press, 1985. After the Holck book, this is an important study.

Planning

Holck, Manfred, Jr. *Annual Budgeting.* Minneapolis: Augsburg Publishing House, 1978.

McDonough, Reginald M. *Leading Your Church in Long-Range Planning.* Convention Press, 1985.

McIntish, Duncan, and R. E. Rusbuldt. *Planning Growth in Your Church.* Valley Forge, Pa.: Judson Press, 1983.

Rusbuldt, R. E.; R. K. Gladden; and N. M. Green. *Key Steps in Local Church Planning.* Valley Forge, Pa.: Judson Press, 1980. Manual of forms included, "Local Church Planning Manual." This is the most important book in this list.

Schaller, Lyle E. *Effective Church Planning.* Nashville: Abingdon Press, 1979.

Walrath, Douglas A. *Planning for Your Church.* Philadelphia: Westminster Press, 1984. This is also a very important study.

Conflict

Leas, Speed. *Leadership and Conflict.* Nashville: Abingdon Press, 1982.

Leas, Speed, and Paul Kittlaus. *Church Fights: Managing Conflict in the Local Church.* Philadelphia: Westminster Press, 1973.

Lewis, Douglas A. *Resolving Church Conflicts.* New York: Harper and Row, 1981.

McSwain, Larry L., and William C. Treadwell, Jr. *Conflict Ministry in the Church.* Nashville: Broadman Press, 1981.

Miller, J. M. *The Contentious Community: Constructive Conflict in the Church.* Philadelphia: Westminster Press, 1978.

Wallace, John. *Control in Conflict.* Nashville: Broadman Press, 1983.

Finance

Crowe, J. M., and Merrill D. Moore. *Church Finance Record System Manual.* Nashville: Broadman Press, n.d.

Hartley, L. H. *Understanding Church Finances.* New York: Pilgrim Press, 1984.

Heyd, Tom. *Accounting Systems for Churches.* Minneapolis: Augsburg Publishing House, 1984.

Holck, Manfred, Jr. *Complete Handbook of Church Accounting.* Englewood Cliffs, N. J.: Prentice-Hall, 1978. Both Holck books are excellent.

———. *Church Finance in a Complex Economy.* Nashville: Abingdon Press, 1983.

Staff

Brown, Jerry W. *Church Staff Teams That Win.* Convention Press, 1979.

Olsen, Frank H. *Church Staff Support: Cultivating and Maintaining Staff Relationships.* Minneapolis: Augsburg Publishing House, 1982.

Rueter, Alvin. *Personnel Management in the Church: Developing Personnel Policies and Practices.* Minneapolis: Augsburg Publishing House, 1984.

Schaller, Lyle. *The Multiple Staff and the Larger Church.* Nashville: Abingdon Press, 1980. This is the most important book in this group.

Wedel, Leonard E. *Church Staff Administration: Practical Approaches.* Nashville: Broadman Press, 1978.

Volunteer Workers

Chartier, Jan. *Developing Leadership in the Teaching Church.* Valley Forge, Pa.: Judson Press, 1985.

Huesser, D. B. *Helping Church Workers Succeed.* Valley Forge, Pa.: Judson Press, 1980.

Johnson, Douglas. *The Care and Feeding of Volunteers.* Nashville: Abingdon Press, 1981.

Jones, R. Wayne. *Using Spiritual Gifts.* Nashville: Broadman Press, 1985.

McDonough, Reginald M. *Working with Volunteer Leaders in the Church.* Nashville: Broadman Press, 1976.

———. *Keys to Effective Motivation.* Nashville: Broadman Press, 1979.

McElvaney, William K. *The People of God in Ministry.* Nashville: Abingdon Press, 1981.

Wilson, Marlene. *How to Mobilize Church Volunteers.* Minneapolis: Augsburg Publishing House, 1983.

Office and Record Management

Mall, E. J. *Handbook for Church Secretaries.* Nashville: Abingdon Press, 1978.

Paulson, Wayne. *Parish Secretary's Handbook.* Minneapolis: Augsburg, 1983.

Tibbetts, Orlando. *How to Keep Useful Church Records.* Valley Forge, Pa.: Judson Press, 1983.

Computers

Bedell, Kenneth. *Using Personal Computers in the Church.* Valley Forge, Pa.: Judson Press, 1982.

Bedell, Kenneth, and Parker Rossman. *Computers: New Opportunities for Personalized Ministry.* Valley Forge, Pa.: Judson Press, 1984.

Johnson, W. R. *Selecting the Church Computer.* Nashville: Abingdon Press, 1984.

Rossman, Parker. *Computers: Bridges to the Future.* Valley Forge, Pa.: Judson Press, 1985.

Church Communication

Craig, Floyd. *Christian Communicator's Handbook.* Nashville: Broadman Press, 1977.

Dunkin, Steve. *Church Advertising.* Nashville: Abingdon Press, 1982.

Williams, Barbara. *Public Relations Handbook for Your Church.* Valley Forge, Pa.: Judson Press, 1985.

Others

Anderton, T. Lee. *Church Property/Building Guidebook.* Convention Press, 1980.

Berghoef, Gerard, and Lester Dekoster. *The Deacons Handbook.* Christians' Library Press, n.d.

————. *The Elder's Handbook.* Christians' Library Press, 1977.

Hammar, Richard R. *Pastor, Church, and Law.* Springfield, Mo.: Gospel Publishing House, 1983.

Myers, Marvin. *Managing the Business Affairs of a Church.* Convention Press, 1981.

Tibbetts, Orlando L. *The Work of the Church Trustee.* Valley Forge, Pa.: Judson Press, 1979.

Index

Due

2/13/18

ı a.m.

Finding the Strength in the of C

11:30 a.m. **Lunch and Laugh** *Stories of your years at*

12:45 a.m. **Brick-laying Ceremony in Memory of P**

Walk of Honor (Front Walkway)

1 p.m. **Forum on Ministry and Marriage** *Lonn*

Discussion (Bill and Laura Bagents, Larry

Thomas ('85) and Marie Holiday) Auditor

3 p.m. **When I'm Tempted to Quit** *Jim Martin*

DAVID S. LUECKE is Vice-President of Seminary Services at Fuller Theological Seminary and is on the faculty of the School of Theology, teaching church administration. An ordained Lutheran minister, he received his Ph.D. in organizational behavior from Washington University. Dr. Luecke and his lawyer wife, Marcia, have three children.

SAMUEL SOUTHARD is Professor of Pastoral Theology at Fuller Theological Seminary, Pasadena, California. He previously served as a pastor and has taught psychology of religion in Southern Baptist Seminary, from which he received his Ph.D. in pastoral theology. His previous books include *Pastoral Evangelism* and *Training Members for Pastoral Care*.